# the household menu and coupon organizer

Revell

*a division of Baker Publishing Group*
Grand Rapids, Michigan

© 2011 by Baker Publishing Group

Published by Revell
a division of Baker Publishing Group
P.O. Box 6287, Grand Rapids, MI 49516-6287
www.revellbooks.com

Printed in China

ISBN 978-0-8007-2018-6

Scripture quotations are from GOD'S WORD®. © 1995 God's Word to the Nations. Used by permission of Baker Publishing Group.

The internet addresses, email addresses, and phone numbers in this book are accurate at the time of publication. They are provided as a resource. Baker Publishing Group does not endorse them or vouch for their content or permanence.

Produced with the assistance of The Livingstone Corporation (www.LivingstoneCorp .com). Project staff includes Linda Taylor and Kelly Barton.

11   12   13   14   15   16   17       7   6   5   4   3   2   1

# Contents

# Welcome

Let's face it. Shopping and meal planning are relentless tasks. We eat three times a day, seven days a week, and it all comes down to you. Some of you love the twin tasks of shopping and meal planning; some of you go in kicking and screaming. It just isn't simple. You are balancing

» family desires (which change as time goes by and tastes change)
» family needs (working around food allergies or special dietary restrictions)
» a desire to give your family healthy food (at least most of the time)
» a need to work within your budget
» your own time constraints
» your own personal limitations (you just might not like to shop and cook)

Still, someone has to do it, and if you're holding this book, chances are that someone is you. That's why we've created *The Household Menu and Coupon Organizer*. Each month includes an article on a shopping or meal-planning topic. These are written by folks who've "been there." Their information and helpful website addresses are in the back of this book for you to peruse for more advice and information at your leisure.

Each month also has a pocket where you can save coupons and recipes you've clipped out of magazines to try "someday." This is followed by a meal-planning chart for the main meal of your day (probably dinner), so there is no more standing in front of the pantry at 5:30 p.m. trying to figure out what to prepare. We also have included a place to plan the food for any special celebrations during the month.

Of course, then you need to go shopping. We've provided for that as well. Four pages for each month include grocery lists with helpful category divisions—four grocery lists for shopping once each week. When you realize you're running low on something, jot it down in the book. As you plan your meals for the month, jot down the ingredients you need to purchase.

Finally, in the back of the book we have included recommended reading along with pages for you to track prices on frequently purchased items to help you get the best deals.

You have your coupons, your menus, and your grocery list all in one place. Grab this book and go! It couldn't be easier.

The Editors

# USDA Dietary Guidelines

What is a healthy diet? The US Department of Agriculture's dietary guidelines describe a healthy diet as one that

» emphasizes fruits, vegetables, whole grains, and fat-free or low-fat milk and milk products
» includes lean meats, poultry, fish, beans, eggs, and nuts
» is low in saturated fats, trans fats, cholesterol, salt (sodium), and added sugars

## Grains

Any food made from wheat, rice, oats, cornmeal, barley, or another cereal grain is a grain product. Bread, pasta, oatmeal, breakfast cereals, tortillas, and grits are examples of grain products. Grains are divided into two subgroups—whole grains and refined grains.

## Fruits and Vegetables

Any vegetable or 100 percent vegetable juice counts as a member of the vegetable group. Any fruit or 100 percent fruit juice counts as part of the fruit group. Vegetables and fruit may be fresh, canned, frozen, or dried.

## Milk Products

All fluid milk products and many foods made from milk are considered part of this food group. Foods made from milk that retain their calcium content are part of the group, while foods made from milk that have little to no calcium—such as cream cheese, cream, and butter—are not. Most milk group choices should be fat-free or low-fat.

## Meat, Poultry, Fish, Beans, Eggs, Nuts

All foods made from meat, poultry, fish, dry beans or peas, eggs, nuts, and seeds are considered part of this group. Dry beans and peas are part of the vegetable group as well. Most meat and poultry choices should be lean or low-fat. Fish, nuts, and seeds contain healthy oils, so choose these foods frequently instead of meat or poultry. Sunflower seeds, almonds, and hazelnuts (filberts) are the richest sources of vitamin E in this food group. To help meet vitamin E recommendations, make these your nut and seed choices often.

## Oils

Oils are fats that are liquid at room temperature, like the vegetable oils used in cooking. Oils come from many different plants and from fish. Foods that are mainly oil include mayonnaise, certain salad dressings, and soft margarine with no trans fats. Most oils are high in monounsaturated or polyunsaturated fats and low in saturated fats. Oils from plant sources (vegetable and nut oils) do not contain any cholesterol. In fact, no foods from plant sources contain cholesterol.

A few plant oils, however, including coconut oil and palm kernel oil, are high in saturated fats, and for nutritional purposes should be considered solid fats. Solid fats are fats that are solid at room temperature, like butter and shortening. Solid fats come from many animal foods and can be made from vegetable oils through a process called hydrogenation.

The preceding information is obtained from www.mypyramid.gov. Check out this website for further information on healthy eating.

# Favorite Family Foods

| Name | Favorite Food | Location of Recipe |
|------|---------------|--------------------|
|      |               |                    |

# Understanding Healthy Eating

There are thousands of books and tens of thousands of websites devoted to the subject of healthy eating, yet often their instructions are more confusing than helpful. Some claim we should abstain from all sugar and fat; others tell us to figure out the calorie count and portion size of every meal, staying within a prescribed range for our body type, etc., etc., etc.

Does this sound like fun to you? No, it sounds more like something that consumes all of the time and energy we'd rather be spending with family and friends, taking care of our home, or relaxing with a good book! So with the wealth of information out there, how does one really come to understand healthy eating?

There are four basic principles that can be applied to anyone regardless of body type, food preference (are you an omnivore or vegetarian?), culture, or food allergies.

1. *Choose foods with one ingredient.* Steak. Oranges. Green peppers. Salmon. Milk. Eggs. Chicken. Butter. Carrots. Are you getting the drift here? In other words, you're going to spend more time picking out fresh ingredients. Why? Fresh equals unprocessed. Fresh means the food is bursting with vitamins and minerals. Fresh allows your body to be healthy.

Since most vegetables and fruits should be consumed within a week after purchase, you'll most likely be stopping at the market once a week for fresh produce.

2. *Make use of your freezer.* We're not saying you should fill it with ice cream and microwave meals! But when fish, chicken, beef, and pork are on sale, you can buy in large quantities if you have a large freezer. You should buy only what you can eat in three months' time. If your only freezer is the small space above the fridge, you can still purchase meat to freeze. In both cases, remove the meat from the store packaging and place in freezer paper or plastic freezer bags and mark on each the contents and the date of purchase. Ideally, you'll be shopping for meats less frequently, so most of your trips to the market will take less time. Having freshly frozen meats and fish will provide you and your family with the necessary protein to stay healthy.

3. *Shop the perimeter of the store.* Only visit the interior shelves for a few items. This sounds strange, right? Well, look back at point number 1. The perimeter of the store is where you will find the fresh foods with one or very few ingredients. The interior shelves, however, are filled with boxed and canned items jam-packed with chemicals that are simply not good for you.

Here's a quick anatomy and physiology lesson. Your liver is meant to remove harmful substances from the body. If you want your liver to do its job well for your entire life, then don't overtax it by making it clean out the chemicals, additives, and preservatives that are found in processed foods. When your liver is unable to do its job, one of the results is unhealthy weight gain.

4. *Eat in moderation.* Too much of anything is never a good thing, and this is especially true of what we put into our bodies. Current studies report that obesity affects about 60 million people in the United States. With more and more prepackaged food and less and less activity, the count of obese folks in the US has

steadily increased since the 1960s.* Moderation is the key here.

One way to keep from overeating is to snack on healthy foods between meals. Keep berries and cut-up veggies in the fridge, along with yogurt and cheese. Have nuts or granola bars on hand.

The guidelines above are just that—a guide for healthy eating. Most of us will, from time to time, indulge in fast food or a boxed meal. But as long as you keep the overprocessed food items to your list of exceptions rather than the norm, you'll be feeding yourself and your family in the healthiest way possible.

## Healthy vs. Unhealthy Ingredients

### Butter vs. Margarine

- » Butter contains cream and sometimes salt.
- » Depending upon the brand, margarine has anywhere from 9 to 17 ingredients, milk being near to last in the list.

### Sugar vs. Artificial Sweeteners

- » Sugar is the only ingredient in itself. It comes from sugar cane (a tall grass with big stems grown in tropical climates) or sugar beet (a root crop grown in the temperate zones of the north).
- » Artificial sweeteners are man-made chemicals that will tax your liver function. One exception is the sweetener made from the stevia plant, the leaves of which can be steeped to add sweetness to drinks or dried and turned into a sweet powder. If you must use an artificial sweetener, the one made with stevia is the healthiest choice.

### Fresh Veggies vs. Canned Veggies

- » Fresh vegetables contain only one ingredient (themselves) and are high in vitamins, minerals, and fiber. It's always wise to wash them well before eating raw or cooking.
- » Canned vegetables lose much of their nutritional value due to their processing, plus artificial colors and preservatives are added, making canned goods the less-than-healthy choice.

### Regular Popcorn vs. Microwave Popcorn

- » Whether you use an air popper or one that stirs the kernels in a little heated oil, you are giving your family a much healthier and satisfying snack than the bag you stick in the microwave. Microwave popcorn is laden with chemicals and salt and gives you far less pop for your buck.

### Fruit Juices

- » Read the labels. If the first or second ingredient is high fructose corn syrup (HFCS), find another juice. HFCS wreaks havoc with blood glucose and insulin levels. Many beverages (especially soda pop) and other processed foods made with HFCS are high in calories and low in nutritional value.

—Carol Chaffee Fielding

*Information gleaned from www.righthealth.com

*My son, pay attention to my words. Open your ears to what I say. Do not lose sight of these things. Keep them deep within your heart because they are life to those who find them and they heal the whole body.*  PROVERBS 4:20–22

# January

## A Mealtime Blessing

May this food restore our strength, giving new energy to tired limbs, new thoughts to weary minds. May this drink restore our souls, giving new vision to dry spirits, new warmth to cold hearts. And once refreshed, may we give new pleasure to you, who gives us all. —Irish blessing

## My Commitment to Good Health during January

This month I will _____

_____

# Dinners for the Month—January

| Week 1 | Week 2 | Week 3 | Week 4 |
|---|---|---|---|
| Sun | Sun | Sun | Sun |
| Mon | Mon | Mon | Mon |
| Tue | Tue | Tue | Tue |
| Wed | Wed | Wed | Wed |
| Thu | Thu | Thu | Thu |
| Fri | Fri | Fri | Fri |
| Sat | Sat | Sat | Sat |

# Parties and Other Celebrations This Month

**Celebration** _____
Date: _____
Menu: _____
_____
_____

**Celebration** _____
Date: _____
Menu: _____
_____
_____

**Celebration** _____
Date: _____
Menu: _____
_____
_____

**Celebration** _____
Date: _____
Menu: _____
_____
_____

# My Grocery List for January, Week 1

**Personal Care**
_____
_____
_____
_____
_____
_____
_____

**Canned Foods**
_____
_____
_____
_____
_____
_____
_____

**Produce**
_____
_____
_____
_____
_____
_____
_____

**Household Items**
_____
_____
_____
_____
_____
_____
_____

**Drinks**
_____
_____
_____
_____
_____
_____
_____

**Meats**
_____
_____
_____
_____
_____
_____
_____

**Breads**
_____
_____
_____
_____
_____
_____
_____

**Snacks**
_____
_____
_____
_____
_____
_____
_____

**Dairy**
_____
_____
_____
_____
_____
_____
_____

**Baking Products**
_____
_____
_____
_____
_____
_____
_____

**Cereals**
_____
_____
_____
_____
_____
_____
_____

**Frozen**
_____
_____
_____
_____
_____
_____
_____

**Condiments**
_____
_____
_____
_____
_____
_____
_____

**Miscellaneous**
_____
_____
_____
_____
_____
_____
_____

**Notes:**
_____
_____
_____
_____
_____
_____
_____

# My Grocery List for January, Week 2

| Personal Care | Canned Foods | Produce |
|---|---|---|
| _____ | _____ | _____ |
| _____ | _____ | _____ |
| _____ | _____ | _____ |
| _____ | _____ | _____ |
| _____ | _____ | _____ |
| _____ | _____ | _____ |
| _____ | _____ | _____ |

| Household Items | Drinks | Meats |
|---|---|---|
| _____ | _____ | _____ |
| _____ | _____ | _____ |
| _____ | _____ | _____ |
| _____ | _____ | _____ |
| _____ | _____ | _____ |
| _____ | _____ | _____ |

| Breads | Snacks | Dairy |
|---|---|---|
| _____ | _____ | _____ |
| _____ | _____ | _____ |
| _____ | _____ | _____ |
| _____ | _____ | _____ |
| _____ | _____ | _____ |
| _____ | _____ | _____ |
| _____ | _____ | _____ |

| Baking Products | Cereals | Frozen |
|---|---|---|
| _____ | _____ | _____ |
| _____ | _____ | _____ |
| _____ | _____ | _____ |
| _____ | _____ | _____ |
| _____ | _____ | _____ |
| _____ | _____ | _____ |
| _____ | _____ | _____ |

| Condiments | Miscellaneous | Notes: |
|---|---|---|
| _____ | _____ | _____ |
| _____ | _____ | _____ |
| _____ | _____ | _____ |
| _____ | _____ | _____ |
| _____ | _____ | _____ |
| _____ | _____ | _____ |

# My Grocery List for January, Week 3

**Personal Care**

**Canned Foods**

**Produce**

**Household Items**

**Drinks**

**Meats**

**Breads**

**Snacks**

**Dairy**

**Baking Products**

**Cereals**

**Frozen**

**Condiments**

**Miscellaneous**

**Notes:**

# My Grocery List for January, Week 4

**Personal Care**
_____
_____
_____
_____
_____
_____
_____

**Canned Foods**
_____
_____
_____
_____
_____
_____
_____

**Produce**
_____
_____
_____
_____
_____
_____
_____

**Household Items**
_____
_____
_____
_____
_____
_____
_____

**Drinks**
_____
_____
_____
_____
_____
_____
_____

**Meats**
_____
_____
_____
_____
_____
_____
_____

**Breads**
_____
_____
_____
_____
_____
_____
_____

**Snacks**
_____
_____
_____
_____
_____
_____
_____

**Dairy**
_____
_____
_____
_____
_____
_____
_____

**Baking Products**
_____
_____
_____
_____
_____
_____
_____

**Cereals**
_____
_____
_____
_____
_____
_____
_____

**Frozen**
_____
_____
_____
_____
_____
_____
_____

**Condiments**
_____
_____
_____
_____
_____
_____
_____

**Miscellaneous**
_____
_____
_____
_____
_____
_____
_____

**Notes:**
_____
_____
_____
_____
_____
_____
_____

# Eating Well Naturally

Nutritious food supplies the raw materials that our body needs to promote growth, repair damage, and provide fuel. Food that God created—real food—does exactly that.

What exactly is "real food"? For the definition, let's get help from someone who knows—someone like your great-grandma. The food she ate was the same as it's been since creation. Obviously, she has a stockpile of culinary wisdom to share with us. For fun, let's refer to her as "Gigi" (short for great-grandma).

## Gigi would say that real food

» consists of whole, unprocessed foodstuffs in three forms: fats, carbohydrates, and protein—all essential for good health.

» comes right from the animal or the ground, as God created it, without going through a processing plant to become devitalized and laden with chemicals, artificial sweeteners, processed sweeteners, antibiotics, synthetic hormones, etc.

» is in short supply in modern supermarkets. Many edibles there are not "good for food."

» spoils, because it doesn't contain chemical preservatives. (But, obviously, it must be eaten before it spoils.)

» will never damage your body but will build, nourish, and repair it. Processed food is damaged food.

» was grown "organically" from creation until about sixty years ago. Chemically grown foods are "the new kid on the block."

## Gigi would also tell you to eat

» breakfast like a king, lunch like a prince, and supper like a pauper. Having fasted about 12 hours upon waking, you need immediate and long-lasting energy for the day. A good "break-fast" provides a hefty serving of calories early in the day so that you have ample time to burn them off. Include a serving of good fat (plenty of butter on your toast) to satiate your hunger for 4 to 6 hours, preventing the need to snack between meals.

» unprocessed fats: butter, tallow, lard, chicken fat, fat from grass-fed cows or goats, coconut and palm oils, and extra-virgin cold-pressed olive oil. Essential for development of hormones, cells, cell membranes, neurotransmitters and more, good fat supplies your body with immediate fuel, allowing you to go longer without feeling hungry or causing weight gain.

» unrefined natural sweeteners such as raw honey, organic maple syrup, palm sugar, and stevia (herbal sweetener)—but eat these in moderation.

» produce grown without chemicals. Safe nonorganic produce includes anything thick-skinned such as citrus fruits, melons, bananas, mangoes, kiwi, pineapple, avocados, and eggplant, as well as sweet corn and asparagus.

» sea or kosher salt, which contains all the macro minerals and dozens of micro minerals that are essential for health.

» healthy protein: fish, seafood, poultry, beef, lamb, game, and eggs that are from pasture-raised animals without antibiotics or steroids.

» cultured foods containing good bacteria, such as whole yogurt and raw sauerkraut.

## Activities

### Pantry Project

Pull out the food you have in your pantry. Look at the ingredients on the labels and record what doesn't sound like "real food" to you. If you want to go further, research those ingredients online.

### Menu Mission

Using your newfound knowledge about real food, develop a menu for one day, including breakfast (large meal), lunch (moderate meal), supper (light meal), and a snack (remember to keep it "real").

### Savings Scheme

There's a bounty of information online about how to eat real food without breaking the bank. Using the search engine on your browser, investigate this aspect of eating real food.

—Sharon Kaufman

*Righteous people flourish like palm trees and grow tall like the cedars in Lebanon. They are planted in the LORD's house. They blossom in our God's courtyards. Even when they are old, they still bear fruit. They are always healthy and fresh.* PSALM 92:12–14

# February

## A Mealtime Blessing

Blessed are you, HaShem, our God, King of the Universe, who brings forth bread from the earth. —Jewish blessing

## My Commitment to Good Health during February

This month I will  _____

_____

# Dinners for the Month—February

| Week 1 | Week 2 | Week 3 | Week 4 |
|--------|--------|--------|--------|
| Sun | Sun | Sun | Sun |
| Mon | Mon | Mon | Mon |
| Tue | Tue | Tue | Tue |
| Wed | Wed | Wed | Wed |
| Thu | Thu | Thu | Thu |
| Fri | Fri | Fri | Fri |
| Sat | Sat | Sat | Sat |

# Parties and Other Celebrations This Month

**Celebration** _____
Date: _____
Menu: _____
_____
_____

**Celebration** _____
Date: _____
Menu: _____
_____
_____

**Celebration** _____
Date: _____
Menu: _____
_____
_____

**Celebration** _____
Date: _____
Menu: _____
_____
_____

# My Grocery List for February, Week 1

| Personal Care | Canned Foods | Produce |
|---|---|---|
| | | |

| Household Items | Drinks | Meats |
|---|---|---|
| | | |

| Breads | Snacks | Dairy |
|---|---|---|
| | | |

| Baking Products | Cereals | Frozen |
|---|---|---|
| | | |

| Condiments | Miscellaneous | Notes: |
|---|---|---|
| | | |

# My Grocery List for February, Week 2

| Personal Care | Canned Foods | Produce |
|---|---|---|
| | | |

| Household Items | Drinks | Meats |
|---|---|---|
| | | |

| Breads | Snacks | Dairy |
|---|---|---|
| | | |

| Baking Products | Cereals | Frozen |
|---|---|---|
| | | |

| Condiments | Miscellaneous | Notes: |
|---|---|---|
| | | |

# My Grocery List for February, Week 3

| Personal Care | Canned Foods | Produce |
|---|---|---|
| | | |

| Household Items | Drinks | Meats |
|---|---|---|
| | | |

| Breads | Snacks | Dairy |
|---|---|---|
| | | |

| Baking Products | Cereals | Frozen |
|---|---|---|
| | | |

| Condiments | Miscellaneous | Notes: |
|---|---|---|
| | | |

# My Grocery List for February, Week 4

| Personal Care | Canned Foods | Produce |
|---|---|---|
| | | |

| Household Items | Drinks | Meats |
|---|---|---|
| | | |

| Breads | Snacks | Dairy |
|---|---|---|
| | | |

| Baking Products | Cereals | Frozen |
|---|---|---|
| | | |

| Condiments | Miscellaneous | Notes: |
|---|---|---|
| | | |

# Budgeting for Groceries

You have a limited amount of cash. Your bills are stacked, and you're not sure how much you should be budgeting for groceries. Overwhelmed to the point of exhaustion, you give up on the good old-fashioned envelope system and try to "spend frugally." Sound all too familiar? If you're struggling with the grocery budget, here are a few suggestions to put you on the right track.

First you need to analyze your historical spending. How much money have you spent on food items in the past month, six months, or year? Look at your financial statements to determine your food expenditures. Be sure to include both grocery shopping and eating out in your calculations. Find your average spending per month and start there.

Next, use that amount as the starting figure for your monthly grocery budget. You can always budget a little extra for eating at restaurants in a separate category. Try reducing your monthly grocery budget by 5 percent every month to gradually find an amount you can be comfortable with for budgeting month after month. Every family's grocery budget will vary, so this is a great formula to follow to eventually determine the right balance between feeding your family and achieving a frugal lifestyle.

Staying on budget will be the most difficult task. Consistency requires a great degree of discipline! Here are some tips for keeping your grocery budget in check:

*Use cash and try budgeting twice a month.* One struggle people often face when budgeting their grocery money is spreading their expenses evenly throughout the month. You may find that you'll spend more cash at the beginning of the month than at the end. The last thing you want to do is go hungry during the last week! Try budgeting for your groceries every two weeks. This will help you overcome the temptation to spend too much at the dawn of a new month.

*Find accountability.* Let others know about your goal to save money on groceries. They will help you stay consistent. Budgeting as a team will ensure that you don't lose your way as you attempt to stick to your plan.

*Answer the "why" question.* Every goal should be developed with a purpose in mind. If you want to stick to a budget, you must first answer why you want to in the first place. Is it so that you can save more money for a major purchase, put away money for your children's education, or invest money in a new business? Without a vision of purpose, your budgeting goals are likely to go nowhere. What are your reasons for saving and budgeting?

Allocating money for food should be the first necessity funded in your personal budget. But that doesn't mean that the grocery budget should be overfunded. Always ask yourself whether or not you truly need a certain grocery item. Following these tips will help you stay on budget and reveal just how far you can stretch your dollar.

Answer the following questions to start the quest to find the perfect grocery budget for you.

| Question | Your Answer |
|---|---|
| Historically, how much money have you spent on food in the last month, six months, or year? | |
| How much money are you spending on groceries versus spending at restaurants? | |
| Who are some people who can help keep you accountable to your grocery budget? | |
| Why is doing a grocery budget important to you? | |
| What actions will you take to ensure you stay on budget (such as an envelope system, twice-a-month budgeting, etc.)? | |

—John Frainee

# March

*Costly treasure and wealth are in the home of a wise person, but a fool devours them.* Proverbs 21:20

## A Mealtime Blessing

We thank the Lord for what we have. For a little more, we would be glad. But as food's so short and times so rough, we thank the Lord we have enough.
—English wartime prayer, 1940

## My Commitment to Good Health during March

This month I will _____

_____

# Dinners for the Month—March

| Week 1 | Week 2 | Week 3 | Week 4 |
|---|---|---|---|
| Sun | Sun | Sun | Sun |
| Mon | Mon | Mon | Mon |
| Tue | Tue | Tue | Tue |
| Wed | Wed | Wed | Wed |
| Thu | Thu | Thu | Thu |
| Fri | Fri | Fri | Fri |
| Sat | Sat | Sat | Sat |

# Parties and Other Celebrations This Month

**Celebration** _____
Date: _____
Menu: _____
_____
_____

**Celebration** _____
Date: _____
Menu: _____
_____
_____

**Celebration** _____
Date: _____
Menu: _____
_____
_____

**Celebration** _____
Date: _____
Menu: _____
_____
_____

# My Grocery List for March, Week 1

**Personal Care**
_____
_____
_____
_____
_____
_____
_____

**Canned Foods**
_____
_____
_____
_____
_____
_____
_____

**Produce**
_____
_____
_____
_____
_____
_____
_____

**Household Items**
_____
_____
_____
_____
_____
_____
_____

**Drinks**
_____
_____
_____
_____
_____
_____
_____

**Meats**
_____
_____
_____
_____
_____
_____
_____

**Breads**
_____
_____
_____
_____
_____
_____
_____

**Snacks**
_____
_____
_____
_____
_____
_____
_____

**Dairy**
_____
_____
_____
_____
_____
_____
_____

**Baking Products**
_____
_____
_____
_____
_____
_____
_____

**Cereals**
_____
_____
_____
_____
_____
_____
_____

**Frozen**
_____
_____
_____
_____
_____
_____
_____

**Condiments**
_____
_____
_____
_____
_____
_____
_____

**Miscellaneous**
_____
_____
_____
_____
_____
_____
_____

**Notes:**
_____
_____
_____
_____
_____
_____
_____

# My Grocery List for March, Week 2

| Personal Care | Canned Foods | Produce |
|---|---|---|
| _____ | _____ | _____ |
| _____ | _____ | _____ |
| _____ | _____ | _____ |
| _____ | _____ | _____ |
| _____ | _____ | _____ |
| _____ | _____ | _____ |
| _____ | _____ | _____ |

| Household Items | Drinks | Meats |
|---|---|---|
| _____ | _____ | _____ |
| _____ | _____ | _____ |
| _____ | _____ | _____ |
| _____ | _____ | _____ |
| _____ | _____ | _____ |
| _____ | _____ | _____ |
| _____ | _____ | _____ |

| Breads | Snacks | Dairy |
|---|---|---|
| _____ | _____ | _____ |
| _____ | _____ | _____ |
| _____ | _____ | _____ |
| _____ | _____ | _____ |
| _____ | _____ | _____ |
| _____ | _____ | _____ |
| _____ | _____ | _____ |

| Baking Products | Cereals | Frozen |
|---|---|---|
| _____ | _____ | _____ |
| _____ | _____ | _____ |
| _____ | _____ | _____ |
| _____ | _____ | _____ |
| _____ | _____ | _____ |
| _____ | _____ | _____ |
| _____ | _____ | _____ |

| Condiments | Miscellaneous | Notes: |
|---|---|---|
| _____ | _____ | _____ |
| _____ | _____ | _____ |
| _____ | _____ | _____ |
| _____ | _____ | _____ |
| _____ | _____ | _____ |
| _____ | _____ | _____ |
| _____ | _____ | _____ |

# My Grocery List for March, Week 3

**Personal Care**
_____
_____
_____
_____
_____
_____
_____

**Canned Foods**
_____
_____
_____
_____
_____
_____
_____

**Produce**
_____
_____
_____
_____
_____
_____
_____

**Household Items**
_____
_____
_____
_____
_____
_____
_____

**Drinks**
_____
_____
_____
_____
_____
_____
_____

**Meats**
_____
_____
_____
_____
_____
_____
_____

**Breads**
_____
_____
_____
_____
_____
_____
_____

**Snacks**
_____
_____
_____
_____
_____
_____
_____

**Dairy**
_____
_____
_____
_____
_____
_____
_____

**Baking Products**
_____
_____
_____
_____
_____
_____
_____

**Cereals**
_____
_____
_____
_____
_____
_____
_____

**Frozen**
_____
_____
_____
_____
_____
_____
_____

**Condiments**
_____
_____
_____
_____
_____
_____
_____

**Miscellaneous**
_____
_____
_____
_____
_____
_____
_____

**Notes:**
_____
_____
_____
_____
_____
_____
_____

# My Grocery List for March, Week 4

| Personal Care | Canned Foods | Produce |
|---|---|---|
| _____ | _____ | _____ |
| _____ | _____ | _____ |
| _____ | _____ | _____ |
| _____ | _____ | _____ |
| _____ | _____ | _____ |
| _____ | _____ | _____ |
| _____ | _____ | _____ |

| Household Items | Drinks | Meats |
|---|---|---|
| _____ | _____ | _____ |
| _____ | _____ | _____ |
| _____ | _____ | _____ |
| _____ | _____ | _____ |
| _____ | _____ | _____ |
| _____ | _____ | _____ |
| _____ | _____ | _____ |

| Breads | Snacks | Dairy |
|---|---|---|
| _____ | _____ | _____ |
| _____ | _____ | _____ |
| _____ | _____ | _____ |
| _____ | _____ | _____ |
| _____ | _____ | _____ |
| _____ | _____ | _____ |
| _____ | _____ | _____ |

| Baking Products | Cereals | Frozen |
|---|---|---|
| _____ | _____ | _____ |
| _____ | _____ | _____ |
| _____ | _____ | _____ |
| _____ | _____ | _____ |
| _____ | _____ | _____ |
| _____ | _____ | _____ |
| _____ | _____ | _____ |

| Condiments | Miscellaneous | Notes: |
|---|---|---|
| _____ | _____ | _____ |
| _____ | _____ | _____ |
| _____ | _____ | _____ |
| _____ | _____ | _____ |
| _____ | _____ | _____ |
| _____ | _____ | _____ |
| _____ | _____ | _____ |

# Getting the Most out of Sales and Coupons

Coupons are one of several ways to save money and, in my opinion, they're the easiest way to do it. Most stores allow you to combine a store coupon with a manufacturer coupon, which gives you double the savings. If your store does not allow you to combine both types of coupons, you will still save tremendously by combining your coupons with store sales.

The pockets in this book are designed to hold the coupons you will need when you go to the store. By writing your weekly grocery list directly in this book and then stashing the matching coupons in that month's pocket, you will have everything you need to save money at the store.

So where can you find coupons? They show up all kinds of places! You can find them in the newspaper, online, at your local grocery store, attached to products, inside product boxes, on receipts, in the mail, and in magazines. Here's a breakdown of the most common types of coupons:

» *Blinkies*. These coupons come out of the little machines with the blinking lights found near certain items in the grocery store.
» *Booklets and Pamphlets*. These contain coupons, recipes, or other product information.
» *Catalinas*. These print at the register. They may also be called checkout coupons and are good "OYNO" (on your next order). Sometimes one will print that is an announcement for an upcoming deal.
» *Peelies*. These are attached to a product.

» *Printables*. Sometimes referred to as IPs, these coupons may be on a company's website. Many can be found at the SmartSource and RedPlum websites. You may need to download a coupon software to print these offers. When you do this, you can take advantage of your love of certain brand-name items. If you love a certain item—say, Mott's Applesauce—check out their website. You might be able to sign up for email specials, often in the form of coupons.
» *Regular Mail*. These often come from signing up for a sample or by contacting the company through their website or phone number.
» *Sunday Inserts*. The Smart Source (SS), Red Plum/Vlassis (RP), and PGBrandSaver (PG) inserts are always found in Sunday newspapers. Often the offers are regional.
» *Tearpads*. These coupons are on a pad near a product on the grocery store shelf.
» *Hang/Winetags*. These coupons hang on a string around a bottle. Check the fine print—not all winetag offers require an alcohol purchase.

So what should you do with all these coupons? It will help immensely if you create a way to organize them at home. You can use the pockets provided in this book, or you might want to use a recipe or index card box with dividers on which you've written various categories (similar to the categories in the boxes on the grocery lists in this book). My preferred method is a coupon binder. I use a three-ring binder with clear baseball-card sleeves and category dividers. This gives me a place to both sort and see all of my coupons.

The key to getting the best deals is to wait until the store has a sale and combine your coupons with the sale. A typical sale cycle is anywhere from six to nine weeks. It will be worth your time to study the sales flyers from your favorite stores each week. After a while, you will begin to see a pattern to the sales cycles and will be able to guess when your favorite items will go on sale. As you study the sales flyers, create your menus based on what is on sale, then match your coupons with the sale items.

Remember to periodically check expiration dates on the coupons. Sort through your stash of coupons and toss the expired ones. That will keep you from getting overwhelmed and save you time and money at the grocery store. After all, if you picked up an item specifically because it was on sale and you had a coupon, if that coupon is expired, would you put the item back? Probably not—so you just lost the saving you thought you had with the coupon.

There are a ton of great deals out there, but it's almost impossible to get them all. Start with one store at a time until you get the hang of it. Make it fun and not stressful. My favorite way to cut coupons is to have my kids help me. They love cutting, plus they get mommy time too!

—Apryl Griffith

*If you search for wisdom as if it were money and hunt for it as if it were hidden treasure, then you will understand the fear of the L*ORD *and you will find the knowledge of God.* PROVERBS 2:4–5

# April

### A Mealtime Blessing

O you who clothe the lilies of the field, and feed the birds of the air, who leads the sheep to pasture and the hart to the water's side, who has multiplied the loaves and fishes and converted the water to wine, do come to our table as giver and guest, to dine. —Old English table prayer

### My Commitment to Good Health during April

This month I will _____

_____

# Dinners for the Month—April

| Week 1 | Week 2 | Week 3 | Week 4 |
|---|---|---|---|
| Sun | Sun | Sun | Sun |
| Mon | Mon | Mon | Mon |
| Tue | Tue | Tue | Tue |
| Wed | Wed | Wed | Wed |
| Thu | Thu | Thu | Thu |
| Fri | Fri | Fri | Fri |
| Sat | Sat | Sat | Sat |

# Parties and Other Celebrations This Month

**Celebration** _____
Date: _____
Menu: _____
_____
_____

**Celebration** _____
Date: _____
Menu: _____
_____
_____

**Celebration** _____
Date: _____
Menu: _____
_____
_____

**Celebration** _____
Date: _____
Menu: _____
_____
_____

# My Grocery List for April, Week 1

**Personal Care**
_____
_____
_____
_____
_____
_____
_____

**Canned Foods**
_____
_____
_____
_____
_____
_____
_____

**Produce**
_____
_____
_____
_____
_____
_____
_____

**Household Items**
_____
_____
_____
_____
_____
_____
_____

**Drinks**
_____
_____
_____
_____
_____
_____
_____

**Meats**
_____
_____
_____
_____
_____
_____
_____

**Breads**
_____
_____
_____
_____
_____
_____

**Snacks**
_____
_____
_____
_____
_____
_____

**Dairy**
_____
_____
_____
_____
_____
_____

**Baking Products**
_____
_____
_____
_____
_____
_____

**Cereals**
_____
_____
_____
_____
_____
_____

**Frozen**
_____
_____
_____
_____
_____
_____

**Condiments**
_____
_____
_____
_____
_____

**Miscellaneous**
_____
_____
_____
_____
_____

**Notes:**
_____
_____
_____
_____
_____

# My Grocery List for April, Week 2

| Personal Care | Canned Foods | Produce |
|---|---|---|
| | | |
| | | |
| | | |
| | | |
| | | |
| | | |

| Household Items | Drinks | Meats |
|---|---|---|
| | | |
| | | |
| | | |
| | | |
| | | |
| | | |

| Breads | Snacks | Dairy |
|---|---|---|
| | | |
| | | |
| | | |
| | | |
| | | |
| | | |

| Baking Products | Cereals | Frozen |
|---|---|---|
| | | |
| | | |
| | | |
| | | |
| | | |
| | | |

| Condiments | Miscellaneous | Notes: |
|---|---|---|
| | | |
| | | |
| | | |
| | | |
| | | |

# My Grocery List for April, Week 3

| Personal Care | Canned Foods | Produce |
|---|---|---|
| | | |

| Household Items | Drinks | Meats |
|---|---|---|
| | | |

| Breads | Snacks | Dairy |
|---|---|---|
| | | |

| Baking Products | Cereals | Frozen |
|---|---|---|
| | | |

| Condiments | Miscellaneous | Notes: |
|---|---|---|
| | | |

# My Grocery List for April, Week 4

**Personal Care**
_____
_____
_____
_____
_____
_____
_____

**Canned Foods**
_____
_____
_____
_____
_____
_____
_____

**Produce**
_____
_____
_____
_____
_____
_____
_____

**Household Items**
_____
_____
_____
_____
_____
_____
_____

**Drinks**
_____
_____
_____
_____
_____
_____
_____

**Meats**
_____
_____
_____
_____
_____
_____
_____

**Breads**
_____
_____
_____
_____
_____
_____
_____

**Snacks**
_____
_____
_____
_____
_____
_____
_____

**Dairy**
_____
_____
_____
_____
_____
_____
_____

**Baking Products**
_____
_____
_____
_____
_____
_____
_____

**Cereals**
_____
_____
_____
_____
_____
_____
_____

**Frozen**
_____
_____
_____
_____
_____
_____
_____

**Condiments**
_____
_____
_____
_____
_____
_____
_____

**Miscellaneous**
_____
_____
_____
_____
_____
_____
_____

**Notes:**
_____
_____
_____
_____
_____
_____
_____

# Gardening Tips

Do you live in an urban or suburban setting and long to move from the city to the country just to have a garden and some chickens? Maybe you already live in the country but have no clue as to how to plot out a little garden of your own. No matter what your living situation, there is hope for those longing to grow their own produce. And the best part is, you don't have to have a green thumb.

In urban and suburban settings there are two excellent alternatives to having a plot of land to garden: community gardens and container gardening.

Community gardens provide access to fresh produce as well as an opportunity to dig in the soil while interacting with neighbors in your community. These gardens are publicly functioning and usually managed by not-for-profit associations. Some are large areas with rows and rows of communally nurtured and equally shared bounty; others have individual plots for personal use. Some are even equipped with raised beds for gardeners with physical limitations or disabilities. To find a community garden near you, visit the American Community Gardening Association online at www.communitygarden.org and see the list of community gardens state by state.

When it comes to container gardening, even the smallest patio, porch, or stoop can boast a garden in containers. Everything from window boxes to large urns can be utilized to grow a bumper crop of vegetables and herbs. Three main ingredients will help the container gardener achieve success: plenty of sunlight, adequate water and drainage, and the proper container to allow the roots to grow. Plants particularly suited to container gardens are herbs, tomatoes, bush beans, peppers, and root vegetables such as carrots and radishes.

If you're blessed with enough lawn space in which a vegetable garden would fit nicely, keep a few things in mind before turning the soil. Although you may have visions of large, lush gardens resembling those that grace the pages of gardening magazines, you really should start small. After a year or two you will be able to better determine what crops you like to raise, how much space is necessary, and whether or not you need to enlarge—or reduce—your garden. Remember, the larger it is, the more time it will consume (weeding, watering, pest control, and picking the produce). And be conservative with the number of plants you include in your garden. Any veteran gardener will tell you that two zucchini plants are more than enough, unless you plan on making zucchini bread for the neighborhood.

Now that you have some ideas of *where* to plant, you're probably wondering *what* to plant. Many gardening websites and longtime gardeners agree that the following list of vegetables are "idiot proof"— perfect for those who don't have a green thumb: beans, squash (especially zucchini), beets, radishes, broccoli, peppers, tomatoes, cucumbers, peas, carrots, onions, pumpkins, many varieties of salad greens, mint, and rhubarb. That's a pretty impressive list!

Most of these can be purchased as small plants at a nursery, so you don't even have to worry about planting seeds and nurturing the seedlings. However, some vegetables that grow quite easily from seed are beans and peas. Also, carrots and radishes should always be planted as seeds directly into the soil and are never available at nurseries as plants. Rhubarb is a gratifying plant to grow because it is a perennial (returns year after year) and is ready to pick before you've even considered planting any other produce in the spring. Mint is also a perennial that needs almost no care and whose leaves make a nice addition to a glass of iced tea.

Consider planting just a few "salad" crops for your first gardening attempt. Small salad greens such as leaf lettuce and spinach mature quickly. Cherry tomatoes, baby carrots, radishes, scallions, spring onions, and green peppers all do well in containers as well as in larger gardens.

These tips should encourage even the most timid gardener to make an attempt at gardening on a small scale. Who knows? The results may surprise you with fresh and delicious additions to your table. There may be some truth to the line in the poem by Dorothy Frances Gurney: "One is nearer God's heart in a garden than anywhere else on earth." Reaching down and picking a fresh vegetable that grew as a result of God's creation and a little work from you will bring joy to the soul.

## Choosing Containers for Container Gardening

Container gardening is limited only to the imagination of the gardener. Depending upon the space available, one can make use of recycled items such as large cottage cheese containers or even plastic kitty-litter containers and five-gallon buckets, or purchase new glazed ceramic pots and hanging baskets. Keep in mind the following guidelines when gardening with containers:

*The size of the container should equal the size of the plant when fully grown.* It's common sense to plant smaller crops in small containers and larger crops in large containers. Carrots would need a planter with a depth of about two inches deeper than the length of the carrot variety you plant. Small containers dry out quickly, so check the soil often and don't let it get dry to the touch.

*Wood planters are susceptible to rot.* Choose a rot-resistant hardwood such as redwood or cedar; avoid wood treated with toxic compounds (creosote, arsenic, etc.), as the vapors can damage the plants and the chemicals can leach into your produce via the plant's roots.

*Thin plastic pots deteriorate and crack easily and are not the best choice for your money.* Terra-cotta pots dry out rapidly, but if you are diligent in watering, they should work fine. Glazed ceramic and heavy plastic pots work the best, but they must have drainage holes. Lining the pot with newspaper prior to adding potting soil will help retain moisture and prevent soil loss through the drainage holes. Be sure pots are raised somewhat (on bricks or trays made for this purpose) to allow free drainage.

*Use light-colored pots in hot climates.* This will lessen heat absorption, reduce uneven root growth, and prevent the soil from drying out. The opposite is true in cooler climates in which heat absorption encourages more growth.

*Hanging baskets should be lined with sphagnum moss to aid in water retention*; still, they will dry out quickly in the sun so be diligent in checking the soil and watering.

—Carol Chaffee Fielding

*Whoever works his land will have plenty to eat.* PROVERBS 28:19

# May

## A Mealtime Blessing

Cristo, pan de vida, Ven y bendice esta comida. Amen.
Christ, bread of life, Come and bless this food. Amen. —Hispanic Lutheran
table prayer

## My Commitment to Good Health during May

This month I will _____

_____

# Dinners for the Month—May

| Week 1 | Week 2 | Week 3 | Week 4 |
|---|---|---|---|
| Sun | Sun | Sun | Sun |
| Mon | Mon | Mon | Mon |
| Tue | Tue | Tue | Tue |
| Wed | Wed | Wed | Wed |
| Thu | Thu | Thu | Thu |
| Fri | Fri | Fri | Fri |
| Sat | Sat | Sat | Sat |

# Parties and Other Celebrations This Month

**Celebration** _____
Date: _____
Menu: _____
_____
_____

**Celebration** _____
Date: _____
Menu: _____
_____
_____

**Celebration** _____
Date: _____
Menu: _____
_____
_____

**Celebration** _____
Date: _____
Menu: _____
_____
_____

# My Grocery List for May, Week 1

**Personal Care**
_____
_____
_____
_____
_____
_____
_____

**Canned Foods**
_____
_____
_____
_____
_____
_____
_____

**Produce**
_____
_____
_____
_____
_____
_____
_____

**Household Items**
_____
_____
_____
_____
_____
_____
_____

**Drinks**
_____
_____
_____
_____
_____
_____
_____

**Meats**
_____
_____
_____
_____
_____
_____
_____

**Breads**
_____
_____
_____
_____
_____
_____
_____

**Snacks**
_____
_____
_____
_____
_____
_____
_____

**Dairy**
_____
_____
_____
_____
_____
_____
_____

**Baking Products**
_____
_____
_____
_____
_____
_____
_____

**Cereals**
_____
_____
_____
_____
_____
_____
_____

**Frozen**
_____
_____
_____
_____
_____
_____
_____

**Condiments**
_____
_____
_____
_____
_____
_____
_____

**Miscellaneous**
_____
_____
_____
_____
_____
_____
_____

**Notes:**
_____
_____
_____
_____
_____
_____
_____

# My Grocery List for May, Week 2

| Personal Care | Canned Foods | Produce |
|---|---|---|
| _____ | _____ | _____ |
| _____ | _____ | _____ |
| _____ | _____ | _____ |
| _____ | _____ | _____ |
| _____ | _____ | _____ |
| _____ | _____ | _____ |
| _____ | _____ | _____ |

| Household Items | Drinks | Meats |
|---|---|---|
| _____ | _____ | _____ |
| _____ | _____ | _____ |
| _____ | _____ | _____ |
| _____ | _____ | _____ |
| _____ | _____ | _____ |
| _____ | _____ | _____ |
| _____ | _____ | _____ |

| Breads | Snacks | Dairy |
|---|---|---|
| _____ | _____ | _____ |
| _____ | _____ | _____ |
| _____ | _____ | _____ |
| _____ | _____ | _____ |
| _____ | _____ | _____ |
| _____ | _____ | _____ |
| _____ | _____ | _____ |

| Baking Products | Cereals | Frozen |
|---|---|---|
| _____ | _____ | _____ |
| _____ | _____ | _____ |
| _____ | _____ | _____ |
| _____ | _____ | _____ |
| _____ | _____ | _____ |
| _____ | _____ | _____ |
| _____ | _____ | _____ |

| Condiments | Miscellaneous | Notes: |
|---|---|---|
| _____ | _____ | _____ |
| _____ | _____ | _____ |
| _____ | _____ | _____ |
| _____ | _____ | _____ |
| _____ | _____ | _____ |
| _____ | _____ | _____ |
| _____ | _____ | _____ |

# My Grocery List for May, Week 3

**Personal Care**
_____
_____
_____
_____
_____
_____
_____

**Canned Foods**
_____
_____
_____
_____
_____
_____
_____

**Produce**
_____
_____
_____
_____
_____
_____
_____

**Household Items**
_____
_____
_____
_____
_____
_____
_____

**Drinks**
_____
_____
_____
_____
_____
_____
_____

**Meats**
_____
_____
_____
_____
_____
_____
_____

**Breads**
_____
_____
_____
_____
_____
_____
_____

**Snacks**
_____
_____
_____
_____
_____
_____
_____

**Dairy**
_____
_____
_____
_____
_____
_____
_____

**Baking Products**
_____
_____
_____
_____
_____
_____
_____

**Cereals**
_____
_____
_____
_____
_____
_____
_____

**Frozen**
_____
_____
_____
_____
_____
_____
_____

**Condiments**
_____
_____
_____
_____
_____
_____
_____

**Miscellaneous**
_____
_____
_____
_____
_____
_____
_____

**Notes:**
_____
_____
_____
_____
_____
_____
_____

# My Grocery List for May, Week 4

| Personal Care | Canned Foods | Produce |
|---|---|---|
| | | |

| Household Items | Drinks | Meats |
|---|---|---|
| | | |

| Breads | Snacks | Dairy |
|---|---|---|
| | | |

| Baking Products | Cereals | Frozen |
|---|---|---|
| | | |

| Condiments | Miscellaneous | Notes: |
|---|---|---|
| | | |

# Navigating Farmers' Markets

If you aren't familiar with farmers' markets, you should know they exist all over the globe, and their produce is renowned for being locally grown and fresh. Because the produce doesn't have to travel as far from the field to your table, it is at the peak of ripeness with the best nutritional content and flavor.

Farmers' markets may also have more than produce; many feature meat, eggs, cheese, raw milk, honey products, syrup, herbs, soaps, and wool. Depending upon where you live, the items found at farmers' markets vary. Some markets are open only "in season," meaning that they are closed when there is no harvest; still others are open year-round, relying upon sales of homemade or locally processed items such as soaps, syrups, fudge, preserves, and even herbal teas.

So now the question is, *when* are farmers' markets stocked with all of their fresh goodies? Again, the answer will vary depending upon your location. For a comprehensive listing of what crops are available in each state every month of the year, visit www.localharvest.org. However, a good rule of thumb for when your local farmers' market will be open is December through April—mid-south and southern states only; May through November—mainly the northern states.

And what comes freshest at what times? The following chart will help (various locales have different produce at different times of the year, so some items are listed more than once):

|  |  |
|---|---|
| **January** | avocados, some citrus fruit |
| **February** | rhubarb |
| **March** | artichokes, asparagus, beets, lettuce/greens, peas |
| **April** | beans, cucumbers, bell peppers, summer squash, turnips |
| **May** | leeks, rhubarb |
| **June** | strawberries, cherries, melons, plums, lettuce/greens, peas, radishes, herbs |
| **July** | sweet corn, peaches, blueberries, beans, summer squash, cucumbers, bell peppers, tomatoes, herbs |
| **August** | sweet corn, tomatoes, asparagus, broccoli, beans, elderberries, onions, herbs, brussels sprouts, hot peppers, acorn squash, dates, figs, potatoes, celery |
| **September** | grapes, apples, pears, cauliflower, wild mushrooms, eggplant |
| **October** | gourds, pumpkins, cranberries, nuts |
| **November** | lettuce/greens |
| **December** | grapefruit and other citrus fruit |

After visiting the farmers' market, many shoppers, whether veterans or newbies, arrive home with bags and bags of produce that goes uneaten. Still others have departed after a morning's tour only to go home with a pint of strawberries and a bewildered expression. Knowing a few rules of etiquette and a bit of planning can make shopping for produce at a farmers' market fun and turn cooking into a delicious adventure.

## Dos of Shopping at a Farmers' Market

*Take your time.* Make a slow loop around the market looking at everything that is offered. Take note of prices and items of special interest.

*Bring cash.* Cash is the easiest currency and is always accepted. Having lots of small bills and a handful of quarters will make sales go more smoothly (sort of like going to garage sales).

*Bring your own bags.* Although some farmers' markets will have bags or boxes, it's best if you have your own reusable containers that will corral blueberries and keep the dirt from those freshly pulled carrots from getting all over your car.

*Bring a cooler.* In hot weather, it would be a shame to have wilted lettuce and squishy raspberries by the time your fresh produce arrives at home.

*Go early.* The best selection is available when the farmers' market opens. And nothing can compare to the colorful sights and fresh fragrances of the just-picked produce.

*Dress for the adventure.* Since most farmers' markets are outdoors—and open in rain or shine—you want to be wearing comfortable shoes and clothing and have an umbrella or sunscreen. If you're bringing children along, make sure they are dressed comfortably and have drinks and snacks while you focus on the produce.

*Ask questions and experiment.* Be sure to ask the farmer when you see something unfamiliar. He or she will be happy to tell you about the produce and how and where it is grown, and may even have some recipes and cooking tips. Additional information on a variety of produce, as well as preparation and recipes, can be found at www.sustainabletable.org.

## Don'ts of Shopping at a Farmers' Market

*Don't whine about the price.* Remember that farmers' markets are not flea markets, and haggling is typically not part of the etiquette. The only exception would be if you plan to buy in bulk (for canning or freezing); then it is acceptable to ask for a discount. Sometimes, just before closing, farmers will offer discounts, but the selection is not the best at that time.

*Don't focus only on the fruit.* Fruit is often more expensive than vegetables. But when vegetables are picked fresh, they are almost as sweet as some of the fruit. If you're watching your wallet closely, feed your sweet tooth some fresh sweet corn, sugar snap peas, or cherry tomatoes.

*Don't forget about the meat, dairy, honey, syrup, soaps, teas, etc.* Farmers' markets often feature local eggs, raw and pasteurized milk, free-range meat, maple syrup, jellies, jams, pies, breads, and other locally made, grown, and processed items. They may be a little more pricey than their chain-store counterparts, but they are more likely to be better for your consumption—more natural ingredients and virtually no chemicals or preservatives.

*Don't squeeze or handle every piece of produce.* Farmers at the market have often harvested their produce at its prime, so it may be soft and easily bruised. Furthermore, overhandling the merchandise is unsanitary—don't pick the produce up to smell it and put it right against your nose.

*Don't let your children run wild.* Ill-behaved children can mix up signs, knock produce on the ground, or stuff food into their mouths. No parent wants to deal with the little one who has stuffed a hot red pepper into her mouth having mistaken it for a strawberry.

*Don't bring pets.* As a general rule, it is not sanitary and may even be illegal to bring a pet into a farmers' market, unless it is a service animal.

—Carol Chaffee Fielding

# June

*Obey my laws, and carefully follow my rules. Then you will live securely in the land. The land will give you its products, and you will eat all you want and live there securely.* LEVITICUS 25:18–19

### A Mealtime Blessing

God is great,
God is good,
And we thank him for our food.
Amen. —Traditional children's mealtime prayer

### My Commitment to Good Health during June

This month I will _____

_____

# Dinners for the Month—June

| Week 1 | Week 2 | Week 3 | Week 4 |
|---|---|---|---|
| Sun | Sun | Sun | Sun |
| Mon | Mon | Mon | Mon |
| Tue | Tue | Tue | Tue |
| Wed | Wed | Wed | Wed |
| Thu | Thu | Thu | Thu |
| Fri | Fri | Fri | Fri |
| Sat | Sat | Sat | Sat |

## Parties and Other Celebrations This Month

**Celebration** _____
Date: _____
Menu: _____
_____
_____

**Celebration** _____
Date: _____
Menu: _____
_____
_____

**Celebration** _____
Date: _____
Menu: _____
_____
_____

**Celebration** _____
Date: _____
Menu: _____
_____
_____

# My Grocery List for June, Week 1

**Personal Care**
_____
_____
_____
_____
_____
_____
_____

**Canned Foods**
_____
_____
_____
_____
_____
_____
_____

**Produce**
_____
_____
_____
_____
_____
_____
_____

**Household Items**
_____
_____
_____
_____
_____
_____
_____

**Drinks**
_____
_____
_____
_____
_____
_____
_____

**Meats**
_____
_____
_____
_____
_____
_____
_____

**Breads**
_____
_____
_____
_____
_____
_____
_____

**Snacks**
_____
_____
_____
_____
_____
_____
_____

**Dairy**
_____
_____
_____
_____
_____
_____
_____

**Baking Products**
_____
_____
_____
_____
_____
_____
_____

**Cereals**
_____
_____
_____
_____
_____
_____
_____

**Frozen**
_____
_____
_____
_____
_____
_____
_____

**Condiments**
_____
_____
_____
_____
_____
_____
_____

**Miscellaneous**
_____
_____
_____
_____
_____
_____
_____

**Notes:**
_____
_____
_____
_____
_____
_____
_____

# My Grocery List for June, Week 2

| Personal Care | Canned Foods | Produce |
|---|---|---|
| _____ | _____ | _____ |
| _____ | _____ | _____ |
| _____ | _____ | _____ |
| _____ | _____ | _____ |
| _____ | _____ | _____ |
| _____ | _____ | _____ |

| Household Items | Drinks | Meats |
|---|---|---|
| _____ | _____ | _____ |
| _____ | _____ | _____ |
| _____ | _____ | _____ |
| _____ | _____ | _____ |
| _____ | _____ | _____ |
| _____ | _____ | _____ |

| Breads | Snacks | Dairy |
|---|---|---|
| _____ | _____ | _____ |
| _____ | _____ | _____ |
| _____ | _____ | _____ |
| _____ | _____ | _____ |
| _____ | _____ | _____ |
| _____ | _____ | _____ |

| Baking Products | Cereals | Frozen |
|---|---|---|
| _____ | _____ | _____ |
| _____ | _____ | _____ |
| _____ | _____ | _____ |
| _____ | _____ | _____ |
| _____ | _____ | _____ |
| _____ | _____ | _____ |

| Condiments | Miscellaneous | Notes: |
|---|---|---|
| _____ | _____ | _____ |
| _____ | _____ | _____ |
| _____ | _____ | _____ |
| _____ | _____ | _____ |
| _____ | _____ | _____ |
| _____ | _____ | _____ |

# My Grocery List for June, Week 3

| Personal Care | Canned Foods | Produce |
|---|---|---|
| | | |

| Household Items | Drinks | Meats |
|---|---|---|
| | | |

| Breads | Snacks | Dairy |
|---|---|---|
| | | |

| Baking Products | Cereals | Frozen |
|---|---|---|
| | | |

| Condiments | Miscellaneous | Notes: |
|---|---|---|
| | | |

# My Grocery List for June, Week 4

| Personal Care | Canned Foods | Produce |
|---|---|---|
| _____ | _____ | _____ |
| _____ | _____ | _____ |
| _____ | _____ | _____ |
| _____ | _____ | _____ |
| _____ | _____ | _____ |
| _____ | _____ | _____ |
| _____ | _____ | _____ |

| Household Items | Drinks | Meats |
|---|---|---|
| _____ | _____ | _____ |
| _____ | _____ | _____ |
| _____ | _____ | _____ |
| _____ | _____ | _____ |
| _____ | _____ | _____ |
| _____ | _____ | _____ |
| _____ | _____ | _____ |

| Breads | Snacks | Dairy |
|---|---|---|
| _____ | _____ | _____ |
| _____ | _____ | _____ |
| _____ | _____ | _____ |
| _____ | _____ | _____ |
| _____ | _____ | _____ |
| _____ | _____ | _____ |
| _____ | _____ | _____ |

| Baking Products | Cereals | Frozen |
|---|---|---|
| _____ | _____ | _____ |
| _____ | _____ | _____ |
| _____ | _____ | _____ |
| _____ | _____ | _____ |
| _____ | _____ | _____ |
| _____ | _____ | _____ |
| _____ | _____ | _____ |

| Condiments | Miscellaneous | Notes: |
|---|---|---|
| _____ | _____ | _____ |
| _____ | _____ | _____ |
| _____ | _____ | _____ |
| _____ | _____ | _____ |
| _____ | _____ | _____ |
| _____ | _____ | _____ |
| _____ | _____ | _____ |

# How Grocery Stores Work

From the moment you set foot in the grocery store, well-placed merchandise begs for your attention. Snacks, trinkets, and all kinds of goodies demand to be purchased immediately. Who can resist the temptations that await in the aisles? Armed with knowledge of the way many grocery stores work, you can keep your food budget in check while finding healthy alternatives.

Grocery stores employ several "traps" to ensure that you will spend more than intended. By understanding these common tactics, you'll find it much easier to grab what you need without being lured by what you want. Consider the following pitfalls:

» *The Bakery:* Bread. We all love it. There's nothing like the smell of warm carbs wafting through the air. The bakery gives you the opportunity to buy more than you really need. Do you really require a dozen donuts? Probably not. If you're trying to rein in your budget, avoid the bakery altogether—unless it's on your list.

» *Endcap Specials:* By placing "specials" on the end of the aisles, marketing professionals trick you into thinking you're getting a great deal. But are you? Dig a little deeper and you'll probably find a box of cereal for less than the "special" that was placed in plain view. Endcaps are typically stocked with comfort food, things that tempt you and beg to be placed in your cart.

» *Coupons:* Yes, even coupons can be a pitfall! Many coupons are printed to encourage customers to spend more. Instead of keeping all coupons, focus on using only the coupons that discount food you were already intending to buy.

» *Free Samples:* Retailers are catching on that priming your taste buds with a free sample encourages spending. One little taste can be the difference between a sale and a missed opportunity. By eating a sample, many people feel obligated to listen to the salesperson's pitch, often grabbing a box before they leave the table. Free samples are not there as a courtesy—they exist because they sell.

» *Distant Essentials:* Think about your local grocery store. Where is the milk? Where are the eggs? Essentials are usually toward the back of the store. Why? You'll have to waltz past a plethora of goods before arriving at what you originally intended to buy. This tactic turns quick trips to the grocery store into shopping sprees.

» *Checkout Splurges:* You've picked up everything you need, and then a wall of chocolate stares you in the face as you wait at the checkout. This is the store's one last chance to compel you to spend more than you originally intended.

As you can see, grocery stores employ a number of strategies to maximize their profit. How can you combat these budget busters? Here are three tips to keep you on the right track:

1. *Make a shopping list.* Allow the list to guide you through the grocery store. When you're making your list, think about essentials and nonessentials. Grocery categories can help—so make use of the ones we've

included in this book, four for each month. Stick to your list and don't cheat!

2. *Practice tunnel vision.* As you walk through the store, pay close attention to where you are looking. Become a person on a mission—don't get distracted! Grocery stores often play soft music to slow your pace. Pop some earbuds in and energize your shopping. Stay focused, grab what you need, check out, and leave in a hurry!

3. *Analyze your trip.* How well did you do? Did you stick to your list? What did you buy that you forgot to write down on your list before you entered the store?

Critique your trip and find ways to make it more concise. Track your spending. Many people find it helpful to use the envelope budgeting system when grocery shopping. As you refine your shopping habits, use less cash. To help you with this, use the table below to track your grocery spending month by month. The goal is to lower your grocery budget while maintaining healthy habits.

Now you're ready. Take your newfound shopping skills and apply them each and every time. Soon you'll be shopping smarter and saving more than you ever thought possible.

| Month | Cash Budgeted | Cash Spent | Notes |
|---|---|---|---|
| | | | |
| | | | |
| | | | |
| | | | |
| | | | |
| | | | |
| | | | |
| | | | |
| | | | |
| | | | |
| | | | |
| | | | |

—John Frainee

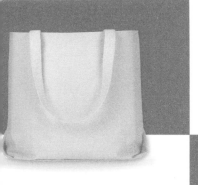

*Keep vanity and lies far away from me. Don't give me either poverty or riches. Feed me only the food I need, or I may feel satisfied and deny you and say, "Who is the LORD?" or I may become poor and steal and give the name of my God a bad reputation.* PROVERBS 30:8–9

# July

### A Mealtime Blessing

Bless, O Lord, the plants, the vegetation, and the herbs of the field, that they may grow and increase to fullness and bear much fruit. And may the fruit of the land remind us of the spiritual fruit we should bear. —Coptic prayer

### My Commitment to Good Health during July

This month I will _____

_____

# Dinners for the Month—July

| Week 1 | Week 2 | Week 3 | Week 4 |
|--------|--------|--------|--------|
| Sun | Sun | Sun | Sun |
| Mon | Mon | Mon | Mon |
| Tue | Tue | Tue | Tue |
| Wed | Wed | Wed | Wed |
| Thu | Thu | Thu | Thu |
| Fri | Fri | Fri | Fri |
| Sat | Sat | Sat | Sat |

# Parties and Other Celebrations This Month

**Celebration** _____
Date: _____
Menu: _____
_____
_____

**Celebration** _____
Date: _____
Menu: _____
_____
_____

**Celebration** _____
Date: _____
Menu: _____
_____
_____

**Celebration** _____
Date: _____
Menu: _____
_____
_____

# My Grocery List for July, Week 1

| Personal Care | Canned Foods | Produce |
|---|---|---|
| | | |

| Household Items | Drinks | Meats |
|---|---|---|
| | | |

| Breads | Snacks | Dairy |
|---|---|---|
| | | |

| Baking Products | Cereals | Frozen |
|---|---|---|
| | | |

| Condiments | Miscellaneous | Notes: |
|---|---|---|
| | | |

# My Grocery List for July, Week 2

**Personal Care**
_____
_____
_____
_____
_____
_____
_____

**Canned Foods**
_____
_____
_____
_____
_____
_____
_____

**Produce**
_____
_____
_____
_____
_____
_____
_____

**Household Items**
_____
_____
_____
_____
_____
_____
_____

**Drinks**
_____
_____
_____
_____
_____
_____
_____

**Meats**
_____
_____
_____
_____
_____
_____
_____

**Breads**
_____
_____
_____
_____
_____
_____
_____

**Snacks**
_____
_____
_____
_____
_____
_____
_____

**Dairy**
_____
_____
_____
_____
_____
_____
_____

**Baking Products**
_____
_____
_____
_____
_____
_____
_____

**Cereals**
_____
_____
_____
_____
_____
_____
_____

**Frozen**
_____
_____
_____
_____
_____
_____
_____

**Condiments**
_____
_____
_____
_____
_____
_____
_____

**Miscellaneous**
_____
_____
_____
_____
_____
_____
_____

**Notes:**
_____
_____
_____
_____
_____
_____
_____

# My Grocery List for July, Week 3

**Personal Care**
_____
_____
_____
_____
_____
_____
_____
_____

**Canned Foods**
_____
_____
_____
_____
_____
_____
_____
_____

**Produce**
_____
_____
_____
_____
_____
_____
_____
_____

**Household Items**
_____
_____
_____
_____
_____
_____
_____
_____

**Drinks**
_____
_____
_____
_____
_____
_____
_____
_____

**Meats**
_____
_____
_____
_____
_____
_____
_____
_____

**Breads**
_____
_____
_____
_____
_____
_____
_____
_____

**Snacks**
_____
_____
_____
_____
_____
_____
_____
_____

**Dairy**
_____
_____
_____
_____
_____
_____
_____
_____

**Baking Products**
_____
_____
_____
_____
_____
_____
_____
_____

**Cereals**
_____
_____
_____
_____
_____
_____
_____
_____

**Frozen**
_____
_____
_____
_____
_____
_____
_____
_____

**Condiments**
_____
_____
_____
_____
_____
_____
_____

**Miscellaneous**
_____
_____
_____
_____
_____
_____
_____

**Notes:**
_____
_____
_____
_____
_____
_____
_____

# My Grocery List for July, Week 4

| Personal Care | Canned Foods | Produce |
|---|---|---|
| _____ | _____ | _____ |
| _____ | _____ | _____ |
| _____ | _____ | _____ |
| _____ | _____ | _____ |
| _____ | _____ | _____ |
| _____ | _____ | _____ |
| _____ | _____ | _____ |

| Household Items | Drinks | Meats |
|---|---|---|
| _____ | _____ | _____ |
| _____ | _____ | _____ |
| _____ | _____ | _____ |
| _____ | _____ | _____ |
| _____ | _____ | _____ |
| _____ | _____ | _____ |
| _____ | _____ | _____ |

| Breads | Snacks | Dairy |
|---|---|---|
| _____ | _____ | _____ |
| _____ | _____ | _____ |
| _____ | _____ | _____ |
| _____ | _____ | _____ |
| _____ | _____ | _____ |
| _____ | _____ | _____ |
| _____ | _____ | _____ |

| Baking Products | Cereals | Frozen |
|---|---|---|
| _____ | _____ | _____ |
| _____ | _____ | _____ |
| _____ | _____ | _____ |
| _____ | _____ | _____ |
| _____ | _____ | _____ |
| _____ | _____ | _____ |
| _____ | _____ | _____ |

| Condiments | Miscellaneous | Notes: |
|---|---|---|
| _____ | _____ | _____ |
| _____ | _____ | _____ |
| _____ | _____ | _____ |
| _____ | _____ | _____ |
| _____ | _____ | _____ |
| _____ | _____ | _____ |
| _____ | _____ | _____ |

# What and How to Stockpile

Stockpiling is buying enough of the items that your family uses the most while they are on sale so that you never have to purchase them at full price. It's not difficult if you follow a few simple steps.

Take a look at your pantry, toiletries, and paper goods. Make a list of what is in your pantry at any given time. These are the items that you need to start stockpiling. For example, if your family eats large quantities of rice and beans, when these go on sale, you should buy as many as you will need until the next time they go on sale (you can learn the cycles of the sales of various items at your favorite stores by watching their circulars). By doing this, you will always have these staples in your pantry, and you'll never have to make that last-minute trip to the grocery store and pay full price.

You need two lists in order to stockpile effectively (see p. 64 for a worksheet to use). The first is a list of the items your family uses most. To figure out what and how much to stockpile, you can record how much of each food and toiletry item your family uses for a couple of months. This should give you a good overview of which items and how much of each to buy. The second list you need is what the rock-bottom prices are in your area. If you find a great deal on an item, write down the price that you spend on it. This will give you a good gauge of the maximum amount that you should spend on this item the next time.

So how much money can stockpiling save you? Let's look at some numbers. If you know that your family eats pasta once a week, then you could buy at least thirty boxes when they are on sale and have enough to feed your family for at least six months. Let's say a box of pasta is $1.59. To buy those thirty boxes at regular price over six months, you would pay $47.70. Some stores often have "buy one, get one free" promotions. You could buy one and get one free and save $1.59. Or, you could buy thirty, pay $47.70, but also *save* $47.70. (You can be sure that most of the other times when you shop for pasta during your regular shopping trips, that sale will not be running.) And that's just one item in your pantry, and a fairly inexpensive one at that. Imagine the savings if you were able to do this with every pantry item, toiletry, and paper good! Granted, you're paying more up front, but once you know the cycles of sales and can budget for one or two stockpile items each time you shop, you'll come out ahead.

When you stockpile, you need to remember a few things.

1. It is very important to *buy only the items that will be used before they reach their expiration date*. Pasta and canned goods may last several months. Check the labels.

2. *Rotate your food in your pantry*. In other words, your recently purchased food does not go at the front of your cupboard. You want to use the oldest first, so place your new groceries either in a different spot or at the back.

3. *Don't change your eating habits in order to stockpile*. Instead, only stockpile the things that your family already enjoys and you know how to cook. It may sound like a wonderful idea to buy ten of one item at a rock bottom price, but if your family won't eat it, then it is just taking up space.

4. *Don't be brand loyal.* If you want rock-bottom prices, you need to be willing to use the brand that is on sale. For instance, if you never want to spend full price on toothpaste, realize that your medicine cabinet will be filled with everything from Crest to Colgate to Arm and Hammer.

5. *Don't forget perishables.* You may not realize that some perishable items can also be stockpiled. You can freeze yogurt, butter, milk, cheese, and meat. With yogurt, freezing does change the texture, but you can use it to make smoothies. Also, butter freezes well; you just need to soften it in the refrigerator the day before you need it. Freezing milk changes the properties a bit, but it can still be used for cooking. Grated cheese freezes well. The best way to purchase meat is to find a local source and split it with another family to reduce your up-front cost.

| | Number Used | Lowest Price |
|---|---|---|
| **Pantry Items** | | |
| | | |
| | | |
| | | |
| | | |
| | | |
| | | |
| | | |
| | | |
| **Toiletry Items** | | |
| | | |
| | | |
| | | |
| | | |
| | | |
| **Paper Goods** | | |
| | | |
| | | |
| | | |
| | | |
| | | |

—Rene Christensen

*Whoever gathers in the summer is a wise son. Whoever sleeps at harvest time brings shame.* PROVERBS 10:5

# August

## A Mealtime Blessing

Bless us, O Lord, and these thy gifts which we are about to receive from thy bounty, through Christ, our Lord. Amen. —Traditional prayer

## My Commitment to Good Health during August

This month I will _____

_____

# Dinners for the Month—August

| Week 1 | Week 2 | Week 3 | Week 4 |
|---|---|---|---|
| Sun | Sun | Sun | Sun |
| Mon | Mon | Mon | Mon |
| Tue | Tue | Tue | Tue |
| Wed | Wed | Wed | Wed |
| Thu | Thu | Thu | Thu |
| Fri | Fri | Fri | Fri |
| Sat | Sat | Sat | Sat |

# Parties and Other Celebrations This Month

Celebration _____
Date: _____
Menu: _____
_____
_____

Celebration _____
Date: _____
Menu: _____
_____
_____

Celebration _____
Date: _____
Menu: _____
_____
_____

Celebration _____
Date: _____
Menu: _____
_____
_____

# My Grocery List for August, Week 1

**Personal Care**

---
---
---
---
---
---
---

**Canned Foods**

---
---
---
---
---
---
---

**Produce**

---
---
---
---
---
---
---

**Household Items**

---
---
---
---
---
---
---

**Drinks**

---
---
---
---
---
---
---

**Meats**

---
---
---
---
---
---
---

**Breads**

---
---
---
---
---
---
---

**Snacks**

---
---
---
---
---
---
---

**Dairy**

---
---
---
---
---
---
---

**Baking Products**

---
---
---
---
---
---
---

**Cereals**

---
---
---
---
---
---
---

**Frozen**

---
---
---
---
---
---
---

**Condiments**

---
---
---
---
---
---

**Miscellaneous**

---
---
---
---
---
---

**Notes:**

---
---
---
---
---
---

# My Grocery List for August, Week 2

| Personal Care | Canned Foods | Produce |
|---|---|---|
| | | |

| Household Items | Drinks | Meats |
|---|---|---|
| | | |

| Breads | Snacks | Dairy |
|---|---|---|
| | | |

| Baking Products | Cereals | Frozen |
|---|---|---|
| | | |

| Condiments | Miscellaneous | Notes: |
|---|---|---|
| | | |

# My Grocery List for August, Week 3

## Personal Care
_____
_____
_____
_____
_____
_____
_____

## Canned Foods
_____
_____
_____
_____
_____
_____
_____

## Produce
_____
_____
_____
_____
_____
_____
_____

## Household Items
_____
_____
_____
_____
_____
_____
_____

## Drinks
_____
_____
_____
_____
_____
_____
_____

## Meats
_____
_____
_____
_____
_____
_____
_____

## Breads
_____
_____
_____
_____
_____
_____
_____

## Snacks
_____
_____
_____
_____
_____
_____
_____

## Dairy
_____
_____
_____
_____
_____
_____
_____

## Baking Products
_____
_____
_____
_____
_____
_____
_____

## Cereals
_____
_____
_____
_____
_____
_____
_____

## Frozen
_____
_____
_____
_____
_____
_____
_____

## Condiments
_____
_____
_____
_____
_____
_____
_____

## Miscellaneous
_____
_____
_____
_____
_____
_____
_____

## Notes:
_____
_____
_____
_____
_____
_____
_____

# My Grocery List for August, Week 4

| Personal Care | Canned Foods | Produce |
|---|---|---|
| _____ | _____ | _____ |
| _____ | _____ | _____ |
| _____ | _____ | _____ |
| _____ | _____ | _____ |
| _____ | _____ | _____ |
| _____ | _____ | _____ |
| _____ | _____ | _____ |

| Household Items | Drinks | Meats |
|---|---|---|
| _____ | _____ | _____ |
| _____ | _____ | _____ |
| _____ | _____ | _____ |
| _____ | _____ | _____ |
| _____ | _____ | _____ |
| _____ | _____ | _____ |
| _____ | _____ | _____ |

| Breads | Snacks | Dairy |
|---|---|---|
| _____ | _____ | _____ |
| _____ | _____ | _____ |
| _____ | _____ | _____ |
| _____ | _____ | _____ |
| _____ | _____ | _____ |
| _____ | _____ | _____ |
| _____ | _____ | _____ |

| Baking Products | Cereals | Frozen |
|---|---|---|
| _____ | _____ | _____ |
| _____ | _____ | _____ |
| _____ | _____ | _____ |
| _____ | _____ | _____ |
| _____ | _____ | _____ |
| _____ | _____ | _____ |
| _____ | _____ | _____ |

| Condiments | Miscellaneous | Notes: |
|---|---|---|
| _____ | _____ | _____ |
| _____ | _____ | _____ |
| _____ | _____ | _____ |
| _____ | _____ | _____ |
| _____ | _____ | _____ |
| _____ | _____ | _____ |

# Healthy Take-Along Lunches

Fall is almost here, and with it comes the last hurrah of bonfires and cookouts, fiery-hued falling leaves, warm Indian summer days and brisk evenings, and of course, kids heading back to school.

Do you dread the thought of attempting to put together healthy bagged lunches for your children (or perhaps yourself or your spouse) once again? Are you feeling uninspired when it comes to affordable, nutritious, and portable meals or snacks?

Packing a health-conscious lunch needn't mean that you turn into a rabbit and munch on lettuce and carrot sticks each day when the clock strikes noon. Nor does it need to cost a fortune at the grocery store or cause undue stress every morning as you prepare to head out the door!

There are a few nutritional basics that should be considered when it comes to making well-balanced lunches:

1. *Protein.* Not only is it crucial for our muscles, cell function, and ensuring that our body has the essential amino acids, it is also a key element for maintaining steady blood-sugar levels throughout the day and sustaining energy levels.

2. *Fiber.* The nutrient that ensures that our bodies run smoothly—it aids in proper digestion, helps to flush toxins out of the blood, and aids in blood-sugar balance.

3. *Hydration.* When the body becomes dehydrated, we feel lethargic, have difficulty focusing, may get headaches, and feel listless and unwell in general. Water is a necessity!

Preparing lunches that contain all of the basics is simple when you use the following strategy for planning. Each lunch should contain:

» Protein-based main item
» Veggie or fruit snack
» Grain or nut snack
» Beverage (water is best)

Creating a weekly schedule will keep things simple and keep you sane. It streamlines your shopping list, as well as your prep time, so you don't spend time racking your brain for what to buy or pack. When you know that you will make the exact same lunch each Tuesday, suddenly packing a lunch on Monday night is a whole lot less daunting.

I suggest making a Monday–Friday schedule, with each day's lunch menu a bit different so that there is variety worked in throughout the course of the week. When you tire of the schedule (maybe in one month or even up to 3 to 4 months), change things up. Keep seasonal food preferences in mind—you might want comfort foods or a warm option during the winter, and lighter, fresher options in spring or summer.

## A Lunchtime Menu Planner

Now it's your turn! Make a list of lunch and snack ideas your family will eat, create your own weekly lunch menu, get the basics you need to pack up your lunches, and then enjoy healthful, hearty, and affordable lunches-to-go this year!

### Main/Protein Item Ideas

Quesadillas, salads with protein (meat, seeds, egg, fish), wraps, cottage cheese, quiche, yogurt (with nuts or fruit), crackers, cheese and meat, hard-boiled eggs, burritos, cold pasta, or rice salad. Thermos options include soups or stews, hot pastas, meatballs.

### Fruit and Vegetable Ideas

Sliced apples or pears, melon/pineapple cubes, oranges (mandarins are easy to peel), bananas, grapes, berries, snap peas, cucumber slices, pepper strips, carrot sticks, broccoli/cauliflower, homemade or 100 percent fruit leather or bars, fruit kabobs, applesauce or pear sauce, guacamole (with veggies or chips to dip), kiwis (with a spoon!), fruit salad, green salads.

### Grain and Nut Ideas

Homemade granola, trail mix (any combo of nuts/seeds/dried fruit), flavored nuts (sweet or savory), homemade muffins, sweet breads (banana, zucchini, pumpkin, etc.), whole-grain crackers, granola bars, nut and seed bars, homemade cookies, corn bread or muffins, air-popped popcorn.

Put it all together by making a weekly lunch menu, like this sample menu:

|  | Monday | Tuesday | Wednesday | Thursday | Friday |
|---|---|---|---|---|---|
| **Main (Protein)** | bean & cheese quesadillas | yogurt/nuts | thermos–soup | bagel sandwich (meat, cheese, lettuce) | cold tuna pasta salad with peas |
| **Fruit & Veggie** | apple and pepper slices | fresh blueberries, green salad | snap peas, mandarin orange | fruit kabob | guacamole, fruit bar |
| **Grains/Nut** | homemade cookie | banana bread | corn muffin | trail mix | whole-grain tortilla chips |
| **Beverage** | water | water | water | water | juice (and water) |

—Stephanie Langford

*She wakes up while it is still dark and gives food to her family.* Proverbs 31:15

# September

### A Mealtime Blessing

Give us grateful hearts, O Father, for all thy mercies, and make us mindful of the needs of others; through Jesus Christ our Lord. Amen. —Book of Common Prayer

### My Commitment to Good Health during September

This month I will _____

_____

# Dinners for the Month—September

| Week 1 | Week 2 | Week 3 | Week 4 |
|---|---|---|---|
| Sun | Sun | Sun | Sun |
| Mon | Mon | Mon | Mon |
| Tue | Tue | Tue | Tue |
| Wed | Wed | Wed | Wed |
| Thu | Thu | Thu | Thu |
| Fri | Fri | Fri | Fri |
| Sat | Sat | Sat | Sat |

# Parties and Other Celebrations This Month

**Celebration** _____
Date: _____
Menu: _____
_____
_____

**Celebration** _____
Date: _____
Menu: _____
_____
_____

**Celebration** _____
Date: _____
Menu: _____
_____
_____

**Celebration** _____
Date: _____
Menu: _____
_____
_____

# My Grocery List for September, Week 1

**Personal Care**
_____
_____
_____
_____
_____
_____
_____

**Canned Foods**
_____
_____
_____
_____
_____
_____
_____

**Produce**
_____
_____
_____
_____
_____
_____
_____

**Household Items**
_____
_____
_____
_____
_____
_____
_____

**Drinks**
_____
_____
_____
_____
_____
_____
_____

**Meats**
_____
_____
_____
_____
_____
_____
_____

**Breads**
_____
_____
_____
_____
_____
_____
_____

**Snacks**
_____
_____
_____
_____
_____
_____
_____

**Dairy**
_____
_____
_____
_____
_____
_____
_____

**Baking Products**
_____
_____
_____
_____
_____
_____
_____

**Cereals**
_____
_____
_____
_____
_____
_____
_____

**Frozen**
_____
_____
_____
_____
_____
_____
_____

**Condiments**
_____
_____
_____
_____
_____
_____
_____

**Miscellaneous**
_____
_____
_____
_____
_____
_____
_____

**Notes:**
_____
_____
_____
_____
_____
_____
_____

# My Grocery List for September, Week 2

| Personal Care | Canned Foods | Produce |
|---|---|---|
| _____ | _____ | _____ |
| _____ | _____ | _____ |
| _____ | _____ | _____ |
| _____ | _____ | _____ |
| _____ | _____ | _____ |
| _____ | _____ | _____ |
| _____ | _____ | _____ |

| Household Items | Drinks | Meats |
|---|---|---|
| _____ | _____ | _____ |
| _____ | _____ | _____ |
| _____ | _____ | _____ |
| _____ | _____ | _____ |
| _____ | _____ | _____ |
| _____ | _____ | _____ |
| _____ | _____ | _____ |

| Breads | Snacks | Dairy |
|---|---|---|
| _____ | _____ | _____ |
| _____ | _____ | _____ |
| _____ | _____ | _____ |
| _____ | _____ | _____ |
| _____ | _____ | _____ |
| _____ | _____ | _____ |
| _____ | _____ | _____ |

| Baking Products | Cereals | Frozen |
|---|---|---|
| _____ | _____ | _____ |
| _____ | _____ | _____ |
| _____ | _____ | _____ |
| _____ | _____ | _____ |
| _____ | _____ | _____ |
| _____ | _____ | _____ |
| _____ | _____ | _____ |

| Condiments | Miscellaneous | Notes: |
|---|---|---|
| _____ | _____ | _____ |
| _____ | _____ | _____ |
| _____ | _____ | _____ |
| _____ | _____ | _____ |
| _____ | _____ | _____ |
| _____ | _____ | _____ |
| _____ | _____ | _____ |

# My Grocery List for September, Week 3

**Personal Care**
_____
_____
_____
_____
_____
_____

**Canned Foods**
_____
_____
_____
_____
_____
_____

**Produce**
_____
_____
_____
_____
_____
_____

**Household Items**
_____
_____
_____
_____
_____
_____

**Drinks**
_____
_____
_____
_____
_____
_____

**Meats**
_____
_____
_____
_____
_____
_____

**Breads**
_____
_____
_____
_____
_____
_____

**Snacks**
_____
_____
_____
_____
_____
_____

**Dairy**
_____
_____
_____
_____
_____
_____

**Baking Products**
_____
_____
_____
_____
_____
_____

**Cereals**
_____
_____
_____
_____
_____
_____

**Frozen**
_____
_____
_____
_____
_____
_____

**Condiments**
_____
_____
_____
_____
_____
_____

**Miscellaneous**
_____
_____
_____
_____
_____
_____

**Notes:**
_____
_____
_____
_____
_____
_____

# My Grocery List for September, Week 4

| Personal Care | Canned Foods | Produce |
|---|---|---|
| _____ | _____ | _____ |
| _____ | _____ | _____ |
| _____ | _____ | _____ |
| _____ | _____ | _____ |
| _____ | _____ | _____ |
| _____ | _____ | _____ |
| _____ | _____ | _____ |

| Household Items | Drinks | Meats |
|---|---|---|
| _____ | _____ | _____ |
| _____ | _____ | _____ |
| _____ | _____ | _____ |
| _____ | _____ | _____ |
| _____ | _____ | _____ |
| _____ | _____ | _____ |
| _____ | _____ | _____ |

| Breads | Snacks | Dairy |
|---|---|---|
| _____ | _____ | _____ |
| _____ | _____ | _____ |
| _____ | _____ | _____ |
| _____ | _____ | _____ |
| _____ | _____ | _____ |
| _____ | _____ | _____ |
| _____ | _____ | _____ |

| Baking Products | Cereals | Frozen |
|---|---|---|
| _____ | _____ | _____ |
| _____ | _____ | _____ |
| _____ | _____ | _____ |
| _____ | _____ | _____ |
| _____ | _____ | _____ |
| _____ | _____ | _____ |
| _____ | _____ | _____ |

| Condiments | Miscellaneous | Notes: |
|---|---|---|
| _____ | _____ | _____ |
| _____ | _____ | _____ |
| _____ | _____ | _____ |
| _____ | _____ | _____ |
| _____ | _____ | _____ |
| _____ | _____ | _____ |
| _____ | _____ | _____ |

# Two Meals from One—Leftovers

On average, American households waste 14 percent of their food purchases. Fifteen percent of that includes products still within their expiration date but never opened. [Anthropologist Timothy W.] Jones estimates an average family of four currently tosses out $590 per year, just in meat, fruits, vegetables, and grain products.*

Are you making use of the food you buy, or do large portions end up being wasted each week? It doesn't have to be this way. There are simple ways you can cut food losses to a minimum and, in the process, save yourself money, time, and energy, not to mention dish cleanup. (I think I caught your attention with that last one!)

There are three primary ways that making good use of leftovers can help you:

## 1. Making Extra

By developing the habit of making most meals larger than your family can eat at one sitting (cooking for 6 to 8 servings instead of 4, for example), you can ensure a steady stream of premade food in the fridge. This is then ready to be utilized for simple lunches or dinners for those really hectic days.

You can make a meal feel slightly different by serving it with a plate of fresh fruit or veggies, sprinkling some shredded cheese on top, adding a bun or slice of bread and butter, or perhaps making a fruit smoothie to drink with it.

_____

* From "The Medical News," http://www.news-medical
.net/news/2004/11/23/6445.aspx

You can use a microwave, but I find that food tastes much better when it's reheated in a stove-top pot, a pan, or an oven (a toaster oven works just fine). It doesn't take much longer this way, and if it makes you want to eat it, then it's worth it!

## 2. Repurposing Leftovers

Perhaps you and your family don't want to eat leftovers. That's fine, because you don't have to, at least not in their original form. Many foods can be used again but in entirely different meals, and you would never know that you were eating, well, you know . . . (shhh, it'll be our little secret). For example:

» Dice leftover baked potatoes. Fried up with eggs the next morning, they make a hearty breakfast.

» Take last night's cooked rice and pan-fry it with oil, some carrots/peas/corn, bits of ham, chicken, or fish (these could also be leftovers), and a scrambled egg or two. Season it with garlic, ginger, and soy sauce. Voila! Fried rice!

» Leftover meat from a pot roast or whole chicken makes for easy fajita or soft-taco filling, can be chopped and added to casseroles or pastas, or can be sliced thinly for sandwiches and wraps.

» Soups and stews are the ultimate vehicle for repurposed leftovers. Rice or barley, beans, lentils, cooked or chopped veggies, any type of meat, poultry, or fish . . . almost any amount of any food (no matter how small) can be worked into a delicious soup, that most versatile of dishes.

## 3. Batch Cooking

Once you've already begun to prepare the ingredients for a meal and dirtied some dishes, it takes little extra time or effort to make double or triple what you are already cooking. If it takes forty minutes to prepare and clean up from one homemade lasagna, it probably only adds another ten minutes to make two instead. That extra investment means that you will have one night the next week when cooking a healthy dinner consists of preheating the oven and popping in a dish!

This can be applied to all sorts of convenience foods that cost a fortune at the grocery store. Mix up a triple batch of whole-wheat waffles on a Saturday morning, and continue to pour batter on the waffle iron as you clean up. You'll be able to stock your freezer with toaster waffles for before-school breakfasts and leave the Eggos on the store shelves.

Try these suggestions and see if you don't love the ease of cooking once and eating twice!

» Batch cook a favorite food and make a plan for using the extras. For example, triple-batch waffles on Saturday morning used as frozen waffles for breakfast on Tuesday and Friday.
» Declare a "buffet dinner" once a week. Clean out the fridge and allow everyone to select their own mix 'n match meal.
» Begin making double of one dinner every week and freezing the extra one for a prep-free meal later on (such as lasagna or pasta, casseroles, soups).
» Get your creative juices flowing. Take a quick inventory of the leftovers that you see, and then come up with a meal that makes good use of them. Ingredient-specific recipes searches (using a website like allrecipes.com) can be really helpful.

—Stephanie Langford

# October

*Each of you as a good manager must use the gift that God has given you to serve others.* 1 PETER 4:10

## A Mealtime Blessing

Some have hunger, but no meat;
Some have meat, but no hunger;
I have both.
God be praised! —A prayer of Oliver Cromwell

### My Commitment to Good Health during October

This month I will _____

_____

# Dinners for the Month—October

| Week 1 | Week 2 | Week 3 | Week 4 |
|---|---|---|---|
| Sun | Sun | Sun | Sun |
| Mon | Mon | Mon | Mon |
| Tue | Tue | Tue | Tue |
| Wed | Wed | Wed | Wed |
| Thu | Thu | Thu | Thu |
| Fri | Fri | Fri | Fri |
| Sat | Sat | Sat | Sat |

# Parties and Other Celebrations This Month

**Celebration** _____
Date: _____
Menu: _____
_____
_____

**Celebration** _____
Date: _____
Menu: _____
_____
_____

**Celebration** _____
Date: _____
Menu: _____
_____
_____

**Celebration** _____
Date: _____
Menu: _____
_____
_____

# My Grocery List for October, Week 1

**Personal Care**
_____
_____
_____
_____
_____
_____
_____
_____

**Canned Foods**
_____
_____
_____
_____
_____
_____
_____
_____

**Produce**
_____
_____
_____
_____
_____
_____
_____
_____

**Household Items**
_____
_____
_____
_____
_____
_____
_____
_____

**Drinks**
_____
_____
_____
_____
_____
_____
_____
_____

**Meats**
_____
_____
_____
_____
_____
_____
_____
_____

**Breads**
_____
_____
_____
_____
_____
_____
_____
_____

**Snacks**
_____
_____
_____
_____
_____
_____
_____
_____

**Dairy**
_____
_____
_____
_____
_____
_____
_____
_____

**Baking Products**
_____
_____
_____
_____
_____
_____
_____
_____

**Cereals**
_____
_____
_____
_____
_____
_____
_____
_____

**Frozen**
_____
_____
_____
_____
_____
_____
_____
_____

**Condiments**
_____
_____
_____
_____
_____
_____
_____
_____

**Miscellaneous**
_____
_____
_____
_____
_____
_____
_____
_____

**Notes:**
_____
_____
_____
_____
_____
_____
_____
_____

# My Grocery List for October, Week 2

| Personal Care | Canned Foods | Produce |
|---|---|---|
| _____ | _____ | _____ |
| _____ | _____ | _____ |
| _____ | _____ | _____ |
| _____ | _____ | _____ |
| _____ | _____ | _____ |
| _____ | _____ | _____ |
| _____ | _____ | _____ |

| Household Items | Drinks | Meats |
|---|---|---|
| _____ | _____ | _____ |
| _____ | _____ | _____ |
| _____ | _____ | _____ |
| _____ | _____ | _____ |
| _____ | _____ | _____ |
| _____ | _____ | _____ |
| _____ | _____ | _____ |

| Breads | Snacks | Dairy |
|---|---|---|
| _____ | _____ | _____ |
| _____ | _____ | _____ |
| _____ | _____ | _____ |
| _____ | _____ | _____ |
| _____ | _____ | _____ |
| _____ | _____ | _____ |
| _____ | _____ | _____ |

| Baking Products | Cereals | Frozen |
|---|---|---|
| _____ | _____ | _____ |
| _____ | _____ | _____ |
| _____ | _____ | _____ |
| _____ | _____ | _____ |
| _____ | _____ | _____ |
| _____ | _____ | _____ |

| Condiments | Miscellaneous | Notes: |
|---|---|---|
| _____ | _____ | _____ |
| _____ | _____ | _____ |
| _____ | _____ | _____ |
| _____ | _____ | _____ |
| _____ | _____ | _____ |
| _____ | _____ | _____ |

# My Grocery List for October, Week 3

**Personal Care**
_____
_____
_____
_____
_____
_____
_____

**Canned Foods**
_____
_____
_____
_____
_____
_____
_____

**Produce**
_____
_____
_____
_____
_____
_____
_____

**Household Items**
_____
_____
_____
_____
_____
_____
_____

**Drinks**
_____
_____
_____
_____
_____
_____
_____

**Meats**
_____
_____
_____
_____
_____
_____
_____

**Breads**
_____
_____
_____
_____
_____
_____
_____

**Snacks**
_____
_____
_____
_____
_____
_____
_____

**Dairy**
_____
_____
_____
_____
_____
_____
_____

**Baking Products**
_____
_____
_____
_____
_____
_____
_____

**Cereals**
_____
_____
_____
_____
_____
_____
_____

**Frozen**
_____
_____
_____
_____
_____
_____
_____

**Condiments**
_____
_____
_____
_____
_____
_____

**Miscellaneous**
_____
_____
_____
_____
_____
_____

**Notes:**
_____
_____
_____
_____
_____
_____

# My Grocery List for October, Week 4

| Personal Care | Canned Foods | Produce |
|---|---|---|
| | | |
| | | |
| | | |
| | | |
| | | |
| | | |

| Household Items | Drinks | Meats |
|---|---|---|
| | | |
| | | |
| | | |
| | | |
| | | |
| | | |

| Breads | Snacks | Dairy |
|---|---|---|
| | | |
| | | |
| | | |
| | | |
| | | |
| | | |

| Baking Products | Cereals | Frozen |
|---|---|---|
| | | |
| | | |
| | | |
| | | |
| | | |
| | | |

| Condiments | Miscellaneous | Notes: |
|---|---|---|
| | | |
| | | |
| | | |
| | | |
| | | |

# Entertaining on a Budget

Entertaining is challenging when your budget is limited. The cost of food, decorations, and party favors can seem like a whizzing lightning bolt that flashes by and burns a big hole in your wallet. It's a good thing there are easy ways to cut costs and still host a memorable event your guests will enjoy!

Food is the essential ingredient when entertaining. Depending on how many guests you are hosting, you may have everything you need already on hand. Instead of planning a menu and shopping accordingly, try a new method. Take inventory of what you have on hand, then plan your menu. If your cupboard is bare, start by choosing an inexpensive focus for your main dish (a cut of meat that is on sale or a vegetarian recipe) and plan around that.

Have your meal almost ready to serve when guests arrive so you won't have to serve too many munchies before mealtime. Choose one simple appetizer such as vegetable dippers with hummus or mini quiches. Both can be made easily and inexpensively from scratch. Prepare dessert with fresh seasonal ingredients. Strawberries from your own garden with homemade vanilla ice cream will please your guests as well as a fancy cake purchased from a bakery.

The cost of beverages can also add up quickly. For formal occasions that require a champagne toast or wine with dinner, shop around for the best price. For more casual affairs, offer one or two drink choices. Offer lemonade and ice-cold bottles of water for a summer gathering. Make a pretty presentation by filling small mason jars with your beverages, then screw the lids on and serve them in a large tub full of ice. In the winter, fill a large slow cooker with apple cider and

another with hot cocoa. Float apple and orange slices studded with cloves in the cider and top the cocoa with whipped cream sprinkled with nutmeg.

When the occasion calls for children's games, keep costs minimal by reaching back to the past for inspiration. Simple games we all remember from childhood like hide-and-seek, sack races, or charades are always fun. Ask guests to bring their favorite board games. During warmer weather, look for great deals on inexpensive outdoor toys at large discount stores. Instead of giving children expensive goody bags, give simple handmade gifts to commemorate the occasion.

When preparing for your guests, create an inviting space as well as appetizing food. Music creates an enjoyable atmosphere. Keep your selections mellow and turn the volume low. Have a variety of CDs on hand to change the mood as you desire, then ask guests to bring their favorites to share as well. Have plenty of seating available and ask family and friends for extra chairs if needed. Prepare serving areas so that guests can easily access utensils, napkins, and trash cans. Arrange extra hand towels, rolls of bath tissue, and hand soap in your guest bathroom to make them easy to find.

Expensive decorations are not necessary when entertaining. Dollar stores have many items that can add flair to your event. A small arrangement of votive candles in glass holders will add elegance to any dinner table. Use small bouquets of silk flowers to replace more costly fresh arrangements. If you must have fresh flowers, cut them from your own garden or glean from a generous neighbor. Use white Christmas lights to add an elegant touch outdoors or when indoor lights are turned low. Shop end-of-summer sales for colorful plastic picnic ware to use throughout the year for casual events. Use the internet to search for party themes, then shop sales fliers to find items that fit the bill at a price you can afford.

Host a potluck for a great way to enjoy your guests without excessive effort. Give your guests a choice of what type of dish to bring (dessert, side dish, salad) or choose a theme (Italian, Mexican, Asian). Then ask the guests to bring copies of their recipes to share. Round out the meal by providing a main dish as well as beverages. Potlucks are especially nice for holidays, bridal showers, and outdoor summer parties.

Creativity is the key to controlling your budget when entertaining guests. To keep costs low, plan things that are simple and informal. No matter what you plan to spend, entertaining will always be a success when guests are kept in mind during planning. If you create a pleasant atmosphere with enjoyable conversation, the size of your budget won't make a difference. Your gathering will be one that your guests remember.

## Entertaining Checklist

*Party Theme* _____     Items to purchase: _____
                                                   _____

### Menu

Appetizer: _____     ### Decorations

Main Dish: _____     Items on hand: _____

Side Dishes: _____   Items to purchase: _____

Dessert: _____

Beverages: _____     ### Game Ideas

Items on hand: _____   _____

_____       _____

### Guest List

| Name | Will Bring |
|---|---|
|  |  |
|  |  |
|  |  |
|  |  |
|  |  |
|  |  |
|  |  |
|  |  |
|  |  |

—Michele Young

*Whoever is generous will be blessed because he has shared his food with the poor.* PROVERBS 22:9

# November

### A Mealtime Blessing

Make us worthy, Lord, to serve those people throughout the world who live and die in poverty and hunger. Give them, through our hands, this day their daily bread, and by our understanding love, give peace and joy. —A prayer of Mother Teresa

### My Commitment to Good Health during November

This month I will _____

_____

# Dinners for the Month—November

| Week 1 | Week 2 | Week 3 | Week 4 |
|--------|--------|--------|--------|
| Sun | Sun | Sun | Sun |
| Mon | Mon | Mon | Mon |
| Tue | Tue | Tue | Tue |
| Wed | Wed | Wed | Wed |
| Thu | Thu | Thu | Thu |
| Fri | Fri | Fri | Fri |
| Sat | Sat | Sat | Sat |

# Parties and Other Celebrations This Month

**Celebration** _____
Date: _____
Menu: _____
_____
_____

**Celebration** _____
Date: _____
Menu: _____
_____
_____

**Celebration** _____
Date: _____
Menu: _____
_____
_____

**Celebration** _____
Date: _____
Menu: _____
_____
_____

# My Grocery List for November, Week 1

**Personal Care**
_____
_____
_____
_____
_____
_____
_____

**Canned Foods**
_____
_____
_____
_____
_____
_____
_____

**Produce**
_____
_____
_____
_____
_____
_____
_____

**Household Items**
_____
_____
_____
_____
_____
_____
_____

**Drinks**
_____
_____
_____
_____
_____
_____
_____

**Meats**
_____
_____
_____
_____
_____
_____
_____

**Breads**
_____
_____
_____
_____
_____
_____
_____

**Snacks**
_____
_____
_____
_____
_____
_____
_____

**Dairy**
_____
_____
_____
_____
_____
_____
_____

**Baking Products**
_____
_____
_____
_____
_____
_____
_____

**Cereals**
_____
_____
_____
_____
_____
_____
_____

**Frozen**
_____
_____
_____
_____
_____
_____
_____

**Condiments**
_____
_____
_____
_____
_____
_____
_____

**Miscellaneous**
_____
_____
_____
_____
_____
_____
_____

**Notes:**
_____
_____
_____
_____
_____
_____
_____

# My Grocery List for November, Week 2

| Personal Care | Canned Foods | Produce |
|---|---|---|
| _____ | _____ | _____ |
| _____ | _____ | _____ |
| _____ | _____ | _____ |
| _____ | _____ | _____ |
| _____ | _____ | _____ |
| _____ | _____ | _____ |
| _____ | _____ | _____ |

| Household Items | Drinks | Meats |
|---|---|---|
| _____ | _____ | _____ |
| _____ | _____ | _____ |
| _____ | _____ | _____ |
| _____ | _____ | _____ |
| _____ | _____ | _____ |
| _____ | _____ | _____ |
| _____ | _____ | _____ |

| Breads | Snacks | Dairy |
|---|---|---|
| _____ | _____ | _____ |
| _____ | _____ | _____ |
| _____ | _____ | _____ |
| _____ | _____ | _____ |
| _____ | _____ | _____ |
| _____ | _____ | _____ |
| _____ | _____ | _____ |

| Baking Products | Cereals | Frozen |
|---|---|---|
| _____ | _____ | _____ |
| _____ | _____ | _____ |
| _____ | _____ | _____ |
| _____ | _____ | _____ |
| _____ | _____ | _____ |
| _____ | _____ | _____ |
| _____ | _____ | _____ |

| Condiments | Miscellaneous | Notes: |
|---|---|---|
| _____ | _____ | _____ |
| _____ | _____ | _____ |
| _____ | _____ | _____ |
| _____ | _____ | _____ |
| _____ | _____ | _____ |
| _____ | _____ | _____ |
| _____ | _____ | _____ |

# My Grocery List for November, Week 3

**Personal Care**
_____
_____
_____
_____
_____
_____
_____

**Canned Foods**
_____
_____
_____
_____
_____
_____
_____

**Produce**
_____
_____
_____
_____
_____
_____
_____

**Household Items**
_____
_____
_____
_____
_____
_____
_____

**Drinks**
_____
_____
_____
_____
_____
_____
_____

**Meats**
_____
_____
_____
_____
_____
_____
_____

**Breads**
_____
_____
_____
_____
_____
_____
_____

**Snacks**
_____
_____
_____
_____
_____
_____
_____

**Dairy**
_____
_____
_____
_____
_____
_____
_____

**Baking Products**
_____
_____
_____
_____
_____
_____
_____

**Cereals**
_____
_____
_____
_____
_____
_____
_____

**Frozen**
_____
_____
_____
_____
_____
_____
_____

**Condiments**
_____
_____
_____
_____
_____
_____
_____

**Miscellaneous**
_____
_____
_____
_____
_____
_____
_____

**Notes:**
_____
_____
_____
_____
_____
_____
_____

# My Grocery List for November, Week 4

| Personal Care | Canned Foods | Produce |
|---|---|---|
| | | |

| Household Items | Drinks | Meats |
|---|---|---|
| | | |

| Breads | Snacks | Dairy |
|---|---|---|
| | | |

| Baking Products | Cereals | Frozen |
|---|---|---|
| | | |

| Condiments | Miscellaneous | Notes: |
|---|---|---|
| | | |

# Stress-Free Holiday Baking

Holiday baking. Just say the words and you immediately imagine your favorite cookies coming out of the oven, the delicious aroma filling the kitchen. You recall the sweet, buttery taste and picture your family sighing with contentment. On the other hand, those same words can cause you to envision a flour-spattered floor, sticky countertops, and a sink filled with dishes. You see burnt cookies, breads that refuse to come out of their pans, and panicked trips to the grocery store for forgotten ingredients.

So which version of holiday baking will appear at your house this year? Let's look at a few ways to make your holiday baking less stressful and more successful. Three easy methods to make the whole experience more enjoyable are: Make a Plan, Make It Ahead, and Make It Fun.

## Make a Plan

Start your holiday baking with a reasonable strategy. Choose wisely what you will bake. Perhaps you remember your mother making twelve different kinds of cookies. But do you really need that many sweets, calories, and extra pounds? It will be healthier and less demanding to choose a few favorites. Perhaps limit yourself to two to four different kinds of cookies. For every difficult or time-consuming cookie (like cut-outs), pick an easier recipe (like bar cookies).

Next, sit down with the recipes you have chosen and list all the ingredients (and the amounts) needed. Check your pantry for what you already have, then make a list of the ingredients you need to buy. On your next regular shopping trip, purchase the ingredients, then hide them or label them "DO NOT USE—FOR CHRISTMAS COOKIES!" so the supplies do not disappear before baking day.

## Make It Ahead

Usually doing something at the last minute makes it more stressful. Fortunately, most holiday treats freeze well, so you can make them ahead, giving you time to enjoy the Christmas pageants and carol-singing sessions.

There are a couple of ways to tackle the baking job. One is to bake one holiday treat each night after supper. Wait to do all the dishes until the cookies are done. Another option is to set aside one day to do all of your baking—that way you have only one day with a messy kitchen.

Here are a few tips for freezing treats:

» Most cookies can be frozen up to three months.
» Freeze cookies in containers with tight-fitting lids.
» Put waxed paper between layers of cookies.
» Store different kinds of cookies in different containers.
» Label containers with the type of cookie and date.
» Thaw at room temperature. Chewy cookies should be thawed in their containers. Cookies meant to be crisp should be removed from the container before thawing.

## Make It Fun

By making it a social activity, baking can be enjoyable. Hosting a cookie exchange is a delicious and fun way to limit your baking. You make only one kind of cookie, but end up with a variety of tasty treats *and* a delightful evening with your friends.

Or plan a baking day to be a fun time with your kids or a friend who likes to bake. Put on some Christmas music and sing while you work.

If you choose to take the one-treat-a-day approach, let each person in the family help with his or her favorite. Use the time to talk about Christmas memories and family traditions.

Finally, balance your work with play. After the baking and cleanup are done, fix a plate of your finished product to eat while you watch a Christmas special with your kids or have a cup of tea with your friend.

Make this holiday season one to remember. Follow these guidelines and the mess and the stress of holiday baking will be a distant memory. Next year you will recall the tastes, the aromas, and the contented sighs.

| Holiday Treat | Recipe Ingredients | Ingredients to Buy |
|---|---|---|
| | | |
| | | |
| | | |
| | | |
| | | |
| | | |
| | | |
| | | |
| | | |
| | | |
| | | |
| | | |
| | | |
| | | |
| | | |
| | | |
| | | |
| | | |
| | | |
| | | |
| | | |

—Sharla Fritz

*A generous person will be made rich, and whoever satis-fies others will himself be satisfied.* PROVERBS 11:25

# December

## A Mealtime Blessing

The eyes of all wait upon thee, O Lord, and thou givest them their food in due season. Thou openest thy hand and fillest all things living with plenteous-ness. —Armenian apostolic prayer

## My Commitment to Good Health during December

This month I will _____

_____

# Dinners for the Month—December

| Week 1 | Week 2 | Week 3 | Week 4 |
|---|---|---|---|
| Sun | Sun | Sun | Sun |
| Mon | Mon | Mon | Mon |
| Tue | Tue | Tue | Tue |
| Wed | Wed | Wed | Wed |
| Thu | Thu | Thu | Thu |
| Fri | Fri | Fri | Fri |
| Sat | Sat | Sat | Sat |

# Parties and Other Celebrations This Month

**Celebration** _____
Date: _____
Menu: _____
_____
_____

**Celebration** _____
Date: _____
Menu: _____
_____
_____

**Celebration** _____
Date: _____
Menu: _____
_____
_____

**Celebration** _____
Date: _____
Menu: _____
_____
_____

# My Grocery List for December, Week 1

**Personal Care**
_____
_____
_____
_____
_____
_____

**Canned Foods**
_____
_____
_____
_____
_____
_____

**Produce**
_____
_____
_____
_____
_____
_____

**Household Items**
_____
_____
_____
_____
_____
_____

**Drinks**
_____
_____
_____
_____
_____
_____

**Meats**
_____
_____
_____
_____
_____
_____

**Breads**
_____
_____
_____
_____
_____
_____

**Snacks**
_____
_____
_____
_____
_____
_____

**Dairy**
_____
_____
_____
_____
_____
_____

**Baking Products**
_____
_____
_____
_____
_____
_____

**Cereals**
_____
_____
_____
_____
_____
_____

**Frozen**
_____
_____
_____
_____
_____
_____

**Condiments**
_____
_____
_____
_____
_____
_____

**Miscellaneous**
_____
_____
_____
_____
_____
_____

**Notes:**
_____
_____
_____
_____
_____
_____

# My Grocery List for December, Week 2

**Personal Care**
_____
_____
_____
_____
_____
_____

**Canned Foods**
_____
_____
_____
_____
_____
_____

**Produce**
_____
_____
_____
_____
_____
_____

**Household Items**
_____
_____
_____
_____
_____
_____

**Drinks**
_____
_____
_____
_____
_____
_____

**Meats**
_____
_____
_____
_____
_____
_____

**Breads**
_____
_____
_____
_____
_____
_____

**Snacks**
_____
_____
_____
_____
_____
_____

**Dairy**
_____
_____
_____
_____
_____
_____

**Baking Products**
_____
_____
_____
_____
_____
_____

**Cereals**
_____
_____
_____
_____
_____
_____

**Frozen**
_____
_____
_____
_____
_____
_____

**Condiments**
_____
_____
_____
_____
_____
_____

**Miscellaneous**
_____
_____
_____
_____
_____
_____

**Notes:**
_____
_____
_____
_____
_____
_____

# My Grocery List for December, Week 3

**Personal Care**
_____
_____
_____
_____
_____
_____
_____

**Canned Foods**
_____
_____
_____
_____
_____
_____
_____

**Produce**
_____
_____
_____
_____
_____
_____
_____

**Household Items**
_____
_____
_____
_____
_____
_____
_____

**Drinks**
_____
_____
_____
_____
_____
_____
_____

**Meats**
_____
_____
_____
_____
_____
_____
_____

**Breads**
_____
_____
_____
_____
_____
_____
_____

**Snacks**
_____
_____
_____
_____
_____
_____
_____

**Dairy**
_____
_____
_____
_____
_____
_____
_____

**Baking Products**
_____
_____
_____
_____
_____
_____
_____

**Cereals**
_____
_____
_____
_____
_____
_____
_____

**Frozen**
_____
_____
_____
_____
_____
_____
_____

**Condiments**
_____
_____
_____
_____
_____
_____
_____

**Miscellaneous**
_____
_____
_____
_____
_____
_____
_____

**Notes:**
_____
_____
_____
_____
_____
_____
_____

# My Grocery List for December, Week 4

| Personal Care | Canned Foods | Produce |
|---|---|---|
| | | |

| Household Items | Drinks | Meats |
|---|---|---|
| | | |

| Breads | Snacks | Dairy |
|---|---|---|
| | | |

| Baking Products | Cereals | Frozen |
|---|---|---|
| | | |

| Condiments | Miscellaneous | Notes: |
|---|---|---|
| | | |

# Recommended Reading

*Don't Panic—Dinner's in the Freezer: Great-Tasting Meals You Can Make Ahead,* Bonnie Garcia, Vanda Howell, and Susie Martinez (Revell, 2005)

*Don't Panic—More Dinner's in the Freezer: A Second Helping of Tasty Meals You Can Make Ahead,* Bonnie Garcia, Vanda Howell, and Susie Martinez (Revell, 2009)

*Healthy Homemaking: One Step at a Time,* Stephanie Langford (Keeper of the Home Publishing, 2009)

*Healthy Meals for Less: Great-Tasting Simple Recipes under $1 a Serving,* Jonni McCoy (Bethany, 2009)

*The Household Money Organizer* (Revell, 2010)

*The Maker's Diet,* Jordan Rubin (Berkley Trade, 2005)

*Nourishing Traditions: The Cookbook That Challenges Politically Correct Nutrition and the Diet Dictocrats,* Sally Fallon (NewTrends Publishing, 1999)

*The Potluck Club Cookbook: Easy Recipes to Enjoy with Family and Friends,* Eva Marie Everson and Linda Evans Shepherd (Revell, 2009)

*Real Food on a Real Budget: How to Eat Healthy for Less,* Stephanie Langford (KOTH Publishing, 2010)

*The Real Food Revival,* Sheri Brooks Vinton and Ann Clark Espuelas (Tarcher, 2005)

*The Reluctant Entertainer: Every Woman's Guide to Simple and Gracious Hospitality,* Sandy Coughlin (Bethany, 2010)

*What the Bible Says about Healthy Living: Three Biblical Principles That Will Change Your Diet and Improve Your Health,* Rex Russell (Regal, 2006)

# Helpful Websites

## From Our Authors

### Rene Christensen

**budgetsavingmom.com**

"Budget Saving Mom" is a helpful blog to assist you in being a good steward of your money. You will find tips on being frugal, free products, coupon sources, gardening advice, instructions for preserving, and more.

### Carol Chaffee Fielding

**livingtheblessing.wordpress.com**

"Living the Blessing" is about finding the joy in every situation, recognizing that we are blessed simply by being alive. Carol covers a wide range of topics, always with an attempt to bring a smile, some new information, or helpful advice to her readers. She welcomes feedback, questions, and suggestions for new topics.

### John Frainee

**thechristiandollar.com**

TheChristianDollar.com is a place where you can explore the world of biblical personal finance. Visit today to learn how you can pay off debt, save money, make wise investments, and give like never before. It's all God's anyway!

### Sharla Fritz

**sharlafritz.blogspot.com**

Sharla loves to communicate Christ's transforming love and grace. Her blog is dedicated to women who are interested in fashion—especially fashion of the soul. It features everything from practical advice on clothing to insight for spiritual style. Sharla's interests extend to money-saving ideas and ways to make life easier for busy women.

### Apryl Griffith

**christianclippers.com**

"Christian Clippers" is a blog dedicated to helping you save money with coupons, bargains, and freebies. It teaches you how to save more so you can give more to others.

### Sharon Kaufman

**franziskaspantry.blogspot.com; the-good-woman.blogspot.com**

The purpose of "Franziska's Pantry" is to offer relevant nutritional information based on traditional diets, the foods that past generations consumed and enjoyed. The information offered here, summed up by one down-to-earth concept—simply eat the real foods that your great-grandmother ate—includes pertinent articles, recipes, food history, menus, and more. Presenting the truth that real food alone supports good health and rebuilds tissue that has been damaged by disease or trauma (something no drug or medical therapy can do), "Franziska's Pantry" challenges readers to pursue a lifestyle of eating real food as a weapon against degenerative disease.

The purpose of "The Good Woman—She's Not Flawless, She's Forgiven" website offers articles pertaining to domesticity (cooking, cleaning, crafts, etc.), marriage, love, biblical womanhood, children, and the Christian woman's relationship with Christ.

## Stephanie Langford

**keeperofthehome.org; savingnaturally.com**

Stephanie has a passion for sharing ideas and information for homemakers who want to make healthy changes in their homes and carefully steward all that they've been given. She has written two books geared to helping families live more naturally and eat real whole foods without being overwhelmed and without going broke. Stephanie is the editor and author of "Keeper of the Home," as well as the site "Saving Naturally," where she helps people to live healthy and spend less.

## Michele Young

**chefmichele.blogspot.com**

Learn how to feed your family nutritious and delicious meals while sticking to your budget. There are lots of menu ideas, recipes, and suggestions for great meals that won't break your bank account.

## Other Helpful Sites

**communitygarden.org**
**localharvest.org**
**righthealth.com**
**stockpilingmoms.com**
**sustainabletable.org**

**stats.bls.gov**

Site for the United States Department of Labor. As a widely used measure of inflation, the Consumer Price Index (CPI) measures price movements for major groups of goods and services. Consumer Expenditures show you how much Americans are spending on items like gasoline and dining out. You may be curious how individuals your age are spending their money. In this table, you can compare your spending habits with the national averages in your group.

**nutrition.gov**

Provides easy, online access to government information on food and human nutrition for consumers. A service of the National Agricultural Library, USDA.

# Price Comparisons

One of our authors, Apryl Griffith ("Getting the Most out of Sales and Coupons"), suggests the following plan for comparing prices at your favorite stores in order to help you locate the best buys in your area:

| Date | Store | Item | Size | Price | Unit Price |
|------|-------|------|------|-------|------------|
|      |       |      |      |       |            |
|      |       |      |      |       |            |
|      |       |      |      |       |            |
|      |       |      |      |       |            |
|      |       |      |      |       |            |
|      |       |      |      |       |            |
|      |       |      |      |       |            |
|      |       |      |      |       |            |
|      |       |      |      |       |            |
|      |       |      |      |       |            |
|      |       |      |      |       |            |
|      |       |      |      |       |            |
|      |       |      |      |       |            |
|      |       |      |      |       |            |
|      |       |      |      |       |            |
|      |       |      |      |       |            |
|      |       |      |      |       |            |
|      |       |      |      |       |            |
|      |       |      |      |       |            |
|      |       |      |      |       |            |

| Date | Store | Item | Size | Price | Unit Price |
|------|-------|------|------|-------|------------|
|      |       |      |      |       |            |
|      |       |      |      |       |            |
|      |       |      |      |       |            |
|      |       |      |      |       |            |
|      |       |      |      |       |            |
|      |       |      |      |       |            |
|      |       |      |      |       |            |
|      |       |      |      |       |            |
|      |       |      |      |       |            |
|      |       |      |      |       |            |
|      |       |      |      |       |            |
|      |       |      |      |       |            |
|      |       |      |      |       |            |
|      |       |      |      |       |            |
|      |       |      |      |       |            |
|      |       |      |      |       |            |
|      |       |      |      |       |            |
|      |       |      |      |       |            |
|      |       |      |      |       |            |
|      |       |      |      |       |            |
|      |       |      |      |       |            |
|      |       |      |      |       |            |
|      |       |      |      |       |            |
|      |       |      |      |       |            |
|      |       |      |      |       |            |